A P

Patrick's Journey Home

- Mark and Elizabeth Matthews -

A Place For Me

Patrick's Journey Home

Foreword by Mark Forrest

RR 4, Box 411
Loogootee IN 47553
www.chelseashire.com

ISBN 0-9748813-0-9
Published by Chelsea Shire Communications, Ltd.
Printed by Country Pines Printing, Inc.

Dedication

We dedicate this book to our mothers, Frances Matthews and Kathleen Gibbons, and to our fathers who have gone before us, Jerome Matthews and Donald Gibbons. Thank you for your love, prayers and guidance that have set us on our own paths toward our heavenly home.

"For we know that if the earthly tent we live in is destroyed, we have a building from God, a house not made with hands, eternal in the heavens."

2 Corinthians 5:1

Contents

Acknowledgments

There are so many people to thank in the production of this book. First, we would like to thank God for giving us the gift of being parents and for our vocation of married life. We would also like to thank our family and friends, both near and far, who have supported us in so many ways throughout our lives. Their love and examples have taught us so much. We would be remiss if we didn't also thank those who have been a great help in writing this book. In particular we thank Bill and Allison Kaiser, Steve and Linda Hullett, Gary and Mary Lowe, Caeser and Jane Swidan, Mark Ginter, and Brittany Somrak.

Foreword

"Behold Satan has demanded to sift all of you like wheat, but I have prayed that your own faith may not fail; and once you have turned back, you must strengthen your brothers."
Luke 22:31-32

Whether or not you are the parent of a special needs child, *A Place for Me* is a book that you just cannot put down. Mark and Elizabeth Matthews open their home and their hearts in this beautiful account of their search to find a special place for their autistic son, Patrick. This search takes them on a fascinating journey as a family, both literally and figuratively, and as they ultimately discover, God is doing the driving!

Raising a child with special needs is both a blessing and a challenge. My wife and I have two sons with special needs, and like the Matthews, we've laughed and cried, questioned ourselves and questioned God, in our search for the narrow path that leads to Him. Like Mark and Elizabeth, we are *all* searching for our "special place" in this world, a place where we can be at peace and be loved and accepted for who we are. We are searching for a place where we can become the people God is calling us to be, no matter what the level of our ability.

This search lasts all of us a lifetime, and the lessons that we learn and relearn along the way dictate where we end up. Many times our "odyssey," as Mark Matthews so aptly describes it, seems to send us in never ending circles. During difficult times in life, we can be very tempted to question God. *Our* solutions seem to make sense to us, whereas the path *He* sometimes sends us on seems long and difficult without direction. That is where our faith makes all the difference.

As Christians we are called to walk by faith and not by sight. If we do this, we are promised everlasting happiness, not in this world, but in the next. What Mark and Elizabeth share so beautifully in *A Place for Me* is that God is simply asking for our blind faith and our obedience. Their honesty in sharing their ups and downs can encourage all of us to keep walking with God, without worrying about where we are going. Life is our journey, the earth our refugee camp in a foreign land. Heaven is our final home and destination. The Matthews family is on that road with all of us, and in this delightfully inspiring and faith-filled book, invite us to share a part of their walk with them.

Our hope is that all of you who leaf through the pages of this book will find words of encouragement and moments of laughter, no matter where you are on your journey to the Lord. For those of you with special needs children, and for those of you with no children, *A Place for Me* will touch your hearts and uplift your spirit. For as the Lord instructed St. Peter many years ago in the garden to strengthen his brothers, so too are Mark and Elizabeth Matthews now strengthening others with their story. Let the journey begin!

God bless,
Mark and Muriel Forrest

Introduction

The past two years since my wife, Beth, wrote *Precious Treasure, The Story of Patrick,* have been an amazing journey for our autistic son, Patrick, and for our family. In January 2001, we thought that Patrick was coming back to our home from Silvercrest, a residential school where he had been living for the previous year. Little did we know that, not only was he not coming home, but also we were headed for quite another adventure. This adventure would lead us through many struggles and up against many obstacles all focused on trying to find the best possible place for Patrick, a place where we could better meet his educational, behavioral, and emotional needs. What we really wanted was for Patrick to be able to come back home with his mom, dad, four brothers, and five sisters. We still want that.

Merriam-Webster defines odyssey as a "long wandering or voyage usually marked by many changes of fortune; an intellectual or spiritual wandering or quest." The past two years with Patrick fits this definition nicely. The journey has been a long wandering marked by many, many changes. It continues to be so. In the midst of this journey, our tenth child, Connor, was born in January, 2002. That May, Emmaus Road published *Precious Treasure.* Beth's book is a collection of letters she wrote to Patrick the first year he was away from us followed by stories of how God has blessed our life with him in beautiful, wondrous ways.

Even though Patrick cannot talk, his story was being told through his mother's words. Beth and I are most grateful to the many people who have told us how touched they were by his story and by our response to his difficulties. I still find it amazing that God is using a non-verbal child to teach others about His goodness and His loving care for us. Patrick's story wasn't finished with *Precious Treasure*, of course. He continues to grow and to change and to challenge us in new, exciting ways.

Most of the changes with Patrick are things we couldn't possibly foresee including changes in his health and behavior. He has experienced many new health problems in the past two years, and his negative behavior has escalated with his frustration at not being able to communicate his needs. Other changes are in areas we had anticipated to a certain extent—the move from elementary to junior high school, physical maturation—but could never prepare for fully.

Our journey also has been an intellectual quest for knowledge and understanding. Beth and I have continued researching autism and related conditions. By no means are we experts, but we have learned much, much more and have sought ways to share this information. The body of knowledge in the study of autism is exhaustive and is growing rapidly. Broadly defined, autism is a communication and social disorder. It's a neurobiological disorder. That is, it's related to brain functioning. It's also a spectrum disorder in that many different symptoms can occur across a wide continuum that includes Asperger Syndrome, Pervasive Developmental Disorder, and variants of both. We discuss autism in various ways throughout the book, but this is not really a book about autism. Certainly Patrick's autism is a big part of our lives, but we hope that all readers can find glimpses of their own journeys and the awesome plan that God has for them throughout *A Place for Me*.

Most importantly, however, our quest has been a spiritual one. God continues to teach us through Patrick, through our other children, and through the circumstances of our lives. It is the greatest of all adventures; our path, we hope, leads to holiness and to heaven. In many respects, it is not a path that we would have chosen, but we have, nevertheless, grown in our acceptance of God's will for our lives.

We have learned, over and over, that God has a place for Patrick and a place for each of us. That place is where we are right now. Tomorrow it may change, but for now we need to do the best we can, where we are, with what we know. Ever since Patrick left us to go to a residential school, we have wanted nothing but for him to be home with us. Allowing Patrick to go to the school was the most heart wrenching and difficult decision we had ever made. Allowing him to continue to live apart from us today is even more difficult. Each day is a struggle. Perhaps someday Patrick will be well enough to be back home with his parents and siblings, but that time is not now. He has so much to learn and so many difficult behaviors to overcome. God alone knows when or if that blessed time will come.

At times Beth will look at me with tears in her eyes and say, "You know, I don't think Patrick's ever coming home." And often I have to agree. Unless God intervenes and performs miracles it is possible she is right, but we simply don't know that. Perhaps someday we will again experience those joys that we had taken for granted. They are the simple joys of having all our children living, growing, studying, working, and praying with us. They are the joys of talking with them at dinner, playing a board game at night, saying prayers, tucking them in bed, kissing them good night, and turning off the lights. It's the joy of knowing our children are safe and sound and not worrying if they are cold, upset, hungry, or lying awake wishing for Mommy or Daddy to soothe them back to sleep. Yes, these are simple joys.

In *A Place for Me,* Beth and I allow you a further glimpse into our lives, and into our hearts. We share our difficulties with Patrick's condition and our desire to find the best possible care for him. Perhaps our struggles seem unique, but I don't think they are. Each of us struggles in some way. All of us have difficulties; all of us bear burdens. God asks us to come to know Him through different circumstances. He tells us in Matthew 10:38 that "anyone who does not take up his cross and follow me is not worthy of me." These crosses are distinctly ours, but we are not alone in this venture. We have the saints to look to for guidance. We have family and friends who are here to support us. We have a community of believers to pray for us and with us. We have Jesus himself who modeled what it means to face life's adversity.

In any case, each of us has a place in this world, but it is far from our permanent home. It is up to us to make the most of what God has bestowed upon us: all our gifts and all our struggles as well. For today we must try to learn what He wants to teach us. For today we must strive to do our best. Yes, we must look to the future and prepare for what may come. Always, though, we must keep our eyes fixed on heaven. St. Paul tells us in 1 Corinthians 15:52 that we will be transformed, "in the twinkling of an eye, at the last trumpet. For the trumpet will sound, the dead will be raised imperishable, and we will be changed." In heaven Patrick will be perfected. He will find his ultimate place. I pray that all of us will find it too. God bless you.

Mark Matthews

A Place for Me

Our dear, sweet son, in your beautiful eyes we can see
You just want to know
Is there a place for me?

My teddy bear's there, but that's not my bed.
Mine is home with my brothers; do they wait for me there?
Mommy, I'm confused. Tell me please.
I want to be home. Is there a place for me?

Who are these people? They come and they go.
What do they want? They frighten me so.
Daddy, I'm scared. Show me please.
I want to be home. Is there a place for me?

This place is loud; it's hurting my ears.
I'm so full of pain from the noise in here.
Mommy, I'm hurting. Comfort me please.
I want to be home. Is there a place for me?

I come home for a visit; we laugh and we play.
Why must I go now? Why can't I stay?
Daddy, I'm lonely. Come get me please.
I want to be home. Is there a place for me?

Come and hold me; I so want a hug.
Wrapped safe in your arms; that's the place that I love.
Mommy, I'm missing you. Come find me please.
I want to be home. Is there a place for me?

In God's hands we've placed you. He will not let go.
Your eyes will be smiling; your tears will be gone.
Soon you'll be there, our dear son
In a place you'll call home.

Elizabeth Matthews

"Whoever receives one such child
in my name receives me."
Matthew 18:5

Chapter One

Home

February 16, 2001

My Dear Patrick,

Today we received a phone call with good news that broke my heart. How can news be both good and heartbreaking at the same time? It seems like such a contradiction. Only through the eyes of faith can it make any sense.

Patrick, for over a year now we have waited for the day you will be coming home. When we first took you to Silvercrest we hoped that you would be there for the minimum stay, only a few months. God had other plans. I know it was hard for you when we took you back after Christmas. We were granted an extension to give us time to find help for you. You are not well enough to come home to stay. Our local school system has told us that they have no extra help to offer you.

The staff at Silvercrest mentioned the possibility of a group home. Those two words ripped at my heart. All I could think of was getting you back home in the safety of my arms. As terrible as it sounded to us, we agreed to look into it. At this point the ones we have tried have told us that they cannot meet your special needs. The news came almost as a relief. We were still clinging to the hope that you would be able to come home.

The months have gone by slowly, and the time for you to come home has already passed. We have weathered many storms together, and I am sure there will be many more. We know you are not ready to be home with us, and yet we want you here so badly. We have prayed daily for God to guide us and to show us where He wants you. As much as we want you with us, we are willing to take you wherever He leads.

The phone call today was from a group home that has a place for you. They want you to live in this new home for a while with a group of boys close to your age. I'm sure the boys will be very special to you, just like your brothers: Sean, Brendan, and Michael. Our hope is that this will provide the perfect transition for you to come back home.

We will pick you up tomorrow to take you to see the house. It may be a little messy because they will be moving in new furniture. The house will be ready soon for you and the other boys. We pray that you will really like it. I wish it were closer to home. In fact, it may take as long to get there as it does to Silvercrest, but it should bring you closer to the time that you can come home for good.

It has been a difficult evening for me, one with many tears. I miss you so much, Patrick. Tomorrow I will hold you in my arms, but until then, as always, I will hold you in my heart. God bless you, my little one.

I love you,
Mommy

"...What no eye has seen, nor ear heard, nor the heart of man conceived, what God has prepared for those who love Him."

1 Corinthians 2:9

After stopping to eat at a North Carolina rest stop, we loaded everyone into the van for the final leg of our 600 mile journey from southern Indiana to see my brother, Greg, my sister, Kathleen, and their families. Greg's family has a beautiful farm in Cary, North Carolina that once was his in-laws' family plantation. It was our first destination on a two-week tour of the Southeast and New England. After several wonderful days of camping on the farm, enjoying backyard cookouts, swimming at their club, chasing peacocks past the tobacco plants, eating homemade ice cream, and riding horses through the pastures, we moved on. We drove up the East coast toward New England, visiting Williamsburg, Jamestown, Ft. McHenry, the Civil War battlefield in Petersburg, Virginia, and several other historical sites and shrines along the way. We visited some friends in Connecticut and Rhode Island and continued north. Our family made our way across New Hampshire to visit the school that our son, Sean, would be attending. Then we crossed through Vermont and upstate New York to the Shrine of the North American Martyrs in Auriesville and on to Niagara Falls. Finally, we were heading home.

It had been a wonderful vacation. It was nearly picture perfect, yet not without its share of storms. Once we stopped at a laundromat in Massachusetts, washed twelve loads of clothes, and then loaded them into the waterproof canvas carrier on top of the van, and drove off into a thunderstorm. Mark and I had a sneaking suspicion that it wasn't really waterproof, and we were right. The next night it was back to another laundromat. There was also the time that my fabulous navigational skills placed us in the Bronx, during rush hour in a thunderstorm. We crept along at five miles per hour across the George Washington Bridge. Mark encouraged the kids to get a long look at New York City and the Hudson because he assured them we were not coming back. Oh yes, we had our share of storms, but realizing it was simply a vacation, we usually were able to laugh about it and move on.

Now as we were heading home, we had one thing and one thing only on our minds, and that was to get back to our little house in southern Indiana nestled up high on a hill between the trees. For some reason we no longer cared about all the things that seemed so important to us at the beginning of our trip. Things like where to eat and what to see didn't matter. Even the noise level in the van didn't bother us any more. We knew it would all be over soon. During long road trips I frequently think of a quote from St. Teresa in which she compares the trials of life with a night in a bad hotel. I would not say that our long drives are comparable to a bad night in a hotel, but they do have their moments.

As we drove through the hilly landscape of southern Indiana toward our home on the last morning of our trip, we had to agree that we were, indeed, driving through the most beautiful place we had seen since leaving home. Certainly, we had seen some pretty spectacular and breathtaking sites like Niagara Falls, a difficult place to visit with not enough big hands to hold little hands. I'm not sure if it was the beauty of the falls that took my breath away, or the fear of one of my little ones getting past the guard rails on their quest for an up close look at the water. Even the lightning from the many thunderstorms we drove through was beautiful at times. I thought to myself, "Why is it that it isn't till the end of our journey that home seems so wonderful and storms so small?"

St. Mary Mackillop of Australia, one of my favorite saints, showed people throughout her life how to endure storms, and that storms would surely strengthen them. Her life was filled with greater trials than many of us could ever imagine. She founded the Sisters of St. Joseph in the late 1800's and faced both excommunication and exile from those who didn't understand her. In one of her letters she wrote, "If we could only remember we are but travelers here. With this thought ever in our minds how easy would the daily trials of life become for us. Great burdens would become great blessings, grace found through adversity." Saint Mary founded the Sisters of St. Joseph to give free education to the poor children of Australia, and yet from the time she was a young girl, Mary had her eyes fixed on heaven, and she knew what really mattered.

It's by God's grace that I have been able to see great trials as blessings. Soon after we learned of Patrick's autism, I was standing in the kitchen with a friend who also has an autistic son a few years older than Patrick. She had come by to drop off some information about different programs that could possibly help Patrick. Before she left, she looked at me and said, "Aren't you angry?" I thought for a moment and said, "No. Why? Should I be?" She then went on to say, "You have to get angry, Beth. You have to mourn the loss of the child that you dreamed of, that you do not have. If you don't, it will destroy you." I knew better. She was simply telling me what she had been told, and what she had been through in her own experiences. My heart went out to her at that moment because I could see in her eyes that she had gone through so much pain.

After my friend left, her words ran through my head over and over again. In my heart I could hear God telling me that He loves Patrick more than I ever could, and that His plans for Patrick are more than I could ever imagine. I had no plans for Patrick other than heaven. After our first son Sean almost died at birth, I realized just how short our time with our children is, and that each day with these children is a gift from God, a gift we do not deserve.

Since that day in the kitchen, several years have passed. Mark and I have traveled many miles with Patrick, stumbling along the way and crying many tears. The storms we have faced have been strong. Some have raged more strongly than others, with gusting winds, pouring rain, blinding lightning and deafening thunder. And through it all God continues to give us strength, showing us glimpses of how awesome His plan is. His beautiful plan will truly lead us home. To heaven.

"Thy kingdom come, thy will be done, on
earth as it is in heaven."
Matthew 6:10

Chapter Two

Mold Me and Make Me

March 17, 2001

Dear Patrick,

Happy St. Patrick's Day! You share a name with a great saint who brought Christianity to Ireland. He was away from home for a long time just like you. His parents probably knew even less about where he was or what he was doing than we know about you. It's so hard to have you away from us. While others are out celebrating their Irish heritage, we're home thinking about you. I hope it has been a special day. I called and talked to John on your floor, and he said you were already asleep. I hope you are having sweet dreams.

I've written a few letters to you, but I don't think I've ever been quite so confused as I am with this letter. Every time I think I know what is best for you things change. I really thought the group home was going to work out for you. Maybe it still will. I just don't know. I do know you haven't been really happy at Silvercrest. You can't tell me anything, but I can see in your eyes when we visit that things just aren't going well for you. It seems like you've been there forever. I don't know what it feels like to you, Patrick, but I feel as if I've been driving that highway to New Albany for much longer than the 15 months you've been there. I know every twist and turn on that curvy road between home and Silvercrest. I figured out the other day that I've driven over 8000 miles to visit you there. I will drive however many miles it takes, Patrick, until we can find some way to make it so you can come back home to us.

Mommy got a phone call a few weeks ago and learned that the group home in Columbus had rejected you. It's the third rejection, Patrick, and we just didn't know what to do. This home seemed like the perfect fit. I wasn't very comfortable with the other two, but this one was so nice. The people were very encouraging. They had observed you at Silvercrest and thought you would be a perfect fit for their house. I even took some digital photographs of the house, your room, and the yard to send to your grandma in California. I had taken some of your things there and had begun to set up the room that was going to be yours. Then you went for the three-day trial, and they took you back to Silvercrest early. The lady on the phone who called Mommy said that they just couldn't provide for your needs there. I didn't understand.

They told us that you needed one on one care around the clock. I have no idea where or how we are ever going to find something like that! Mom called everyone she could think to call. It was one big, wild goose chase. She talked to the social worker at your school, the state department for family and social services, the Bureau of Developmental Disabilities, and the local schools. No one seemed to know how to help you. It was one maddening circle for her as one person after another referred Mommy to another agency. Eventually, they referred her right back where she started. I asked Silvercrest for another extension so we could figure out what to do for you, but they have rejected it. I think they have someone waiting for your spot when you leave, and I can appreciate that. It's so hard though, Patrick. Mommy and I feel like we are doing everything we can to provide what is best for you, but we keep getting rejected and don't know where to turn.

After Silvercrest rejected your extension I called a good friend of mine from Carmel. He has a special son like you too, Patrick. After talking to him, Mommy and I decided that there was only one thing we could do. We ended up filing a due process lawsuit against your school so that they would keep you until we can get this whole mess figured out. I hate to put you in the middle of controversy, Patrick, but I just don't know what else to do. Mommy and I have been praying and begging God to lead us in the direction we need to go. We've never stopped praying for you, Patrick. Every day I pray that you will be healed and can come back home again so that our whole family can be together. I don't know why God thinks that we need to be apart now, but I will accept it. I know He has some awesome plan for you. I just don't know what it is.

Patrick, next week we are going to meet with a couple in Indianapolis. We met with them one other time just after the last group home rejected you. He's an attorney who specializes in helping children like you. She's an advocate for special needs children. Some friends referred us to them, and they were the ones who helped us file the lawsuit. They say they have some great ideas that could really help you. I have no idea what is going to happen, but I trust that God will not abandon us. I miss you so much, and I want to be with you, Patrick. I wish there were some way that I could get you to understand how much I love you and how badly I want you to come home. I pray that your guardian angel keeps you safe and that you will be happy until I can see you again. It won't be long until Spring Break. I can't wait to give you a big bear hug and that deep pressure you so badly crave. Maybe by then we will have this all figured out. Wouldn't that be great? There is always hope, Patrick.

I love you,
Daddy

"O the depth of the riches and wisdom and knowledge of God! How unsearchable are his judgments and how inscrutable his ways!

Romans 11:33

I have always liked Eddie Espinosa's song "Change My Heart, O God." I first heard it at a youth conference at Franciscan University in Steubenville, Ohio in the early 1990's. One of the verses says, "You are the potter. I am the clay. Mold me and make me. This is what I pray." As a young boy I always loved playing in my sandbox or at the beach, wetting the sand down and forming it into various configurations. I wish you could have seen the castles, forts, and cities I constructed! As a grade school student, my favorite activity in art class was working with Play-Doh or modeling clay. I loved the feel of it in my hands, the shapes I could make, and even the slightly salty taste the clay left on my fingers.

Of course the molding in "Change My Heart, O God" isn't child's play. It is God transforming our very souls. While I really liked the song from the very beginning, I didn't think too deeply about the words for a long time. Usually when I like a song for the rhythm or beat I don't think too much about the lyrics until I find myself unknowingly singing along one day. That gets me into trouble when it's a song by someone like AC/DC, especially when they are singing about being on the highway to hell. In Espinosa's song, however, I got into trouble in a completely different way. In the song we are telling God that we want to be molded into whatever image He desires for us. If I really believe the words of that song, then I must be willing to be molded into a new image or even refined by fire if that is what it takes.

Frequently, I resist God's molding. I am far too comfortable the way I am, in my faults and in my sins. It seems that I'm always making the same mistakes despite my best efforts to change. It takes a sincere effort of my will to allow God to prod me, poke me, and ultimately change me into what He desires. Slowly over time I have been more willing to allow Him to do it, but I have sometimes been very resistant.

Patrick is different. He has enjoyed being prodded and pressured. It's not so much that he wants to be changed. I don't think he's too aware of that. Instead, he simply likes deep pressure. It is one of his many sensory needs. Patrick has always craved the pressure of someone hugging him deeply. When he was younger, he would get that pressure any way he could. Sometimes he would slide in behind someone sitting on the couch and pull that person back toward him. Often he would climb under couch cushions or wedge himself into tight spots. He also loved wrestling on the floor with me and would even try to pull me on top of him.

Still other times he would drop onto his head from tabletops or while sliding headfirst down the stairs. Patrick also seemed to enjoy jumping off things and feeling the sensation of his legs crashing into the floor or ground. When he was about two and a half, he would often jump from the top bunk of his bed. These were not your ordinary kid-sized bunk beds either. I had made them during one Lent to Beth's design, about eighteen inches taller than normal bunk beds. Once Beth heard a repeated thudding sound from the kitchen. She knew that was not a good sound in a home full of toddlers, so she went upstairs to investigate. Sean, who was nearly five at the time, cheerfully reported, "Mom, I've been counting. That's the fifth time Patrick has climbed up and jumped out of the top bunk of his bed."

I had no idea why Patrick did these things, but I also had no idea how to stop him from doing them, of even if I should stop him. Later, autism specialists confirmed that he was seeking the deep pressure that these activities provided. They actually have a calming effect on him. It was very tricky, however, because, even though he craved the pressure, he frequently couldn't tolerate the touch of other people. I know it doesn't make sense, but as much as he enjoyed the deep pressure, I could also see that it was all he could do at times to allow himself to be hugged. It may have been the smell of someone's cologne, the feel of his or her clothing, or the texture of one's skin that made it difficult. Nonetheless, he craved the pressure so much that he was often willing to put up with the accompanying discomforts.

Temple Grandin, a noted writer and speaker who happens to be autistic, has shed a lot of light on this subject and others. She has earned a Ph.D. in Animal Science from the University of Illinois and has designed systems for a more humane slaughter of cattle. In fact, almost half of the cattle in North America are handled in systems that she has designed. Her book *Emergence: Labelled Autistic* broke a lot of ground when it was published in 1986. In that book and a second, *Thinking in Pictures*, Grandin discusses what autism is like for her. Granted, she is very highly intelligent and very high functioning, but most agree that there are similarities between her experiences and those of other autistic people. Grandin talks about the need she has had for deep pressure throughout her life and also the repulsion she often felt when someone tried to hug her or was too close to her. To fill her own need for this pressure she created a "squeeze machine." She could cocoon herself into this device and could regulate the amount of pressure it applied. It was her own experience with the calming effects of this pressure that allowed her to develop the processing systems for cattle that keep the animals calmer on their way to slaughter. I am so thankful that Dr. Grandin has shared from her experiences because it has given me some precious glimpses into what may be going on inside Patrick's mind.

As Patrick is non-verbal, he has had no way to express his need for the deep pressure except to attempt to provide it for himself in whatever ways he could. This desire led him into a precarious situation when he was ten. We had moved into a new home and were modifying it to try to better meet Patrick's needs. As usual it was a struggle to try to make our home work for him, and so we decided to build on to our house much as we had done in our previous home. Part of the addition was a basement room designed to be Patrick's bedroom. After the basement walls and floor were poured, but before we had built above it, Patrick decided to meet a more immediate need and jumped into the basement, a distance of eight feet. It was easy for him to get in, but it wasn't going to be so easy to get out. Beth was about six months pregnant with our ninth child, Emily, and there was no way she could get down in the hole to get him. None of the other kids could lift my ladders to try to retrieve him, so he was stuck there for a couple hours until I came home from work.

Rarely was Patrick as safe as he was in his pit. There was no doubt about where he was; he couldn't get hurt, and he certainly wasn't going to run away. That was about as much as we could ever ask for, but, of course, Patrick couldn't stay there. Some of his brothers and sisters were nice enough to throw a few toys to him, and Kate even threw a few pieces of gravel that Patrick promptly used as chalk to draw on the cement walls.

As I pulled my ladder across the muddy yard to free Patrick from his open-aired dungeon, I was struck with what he had put himself through. I know he thought it was a great idea at the time. He must have known that he would like the feeling of jumping onto the hard surface from above. I imagine his thoughts went no further than that. I had to laugh when I looked down at him and asked him if he was ready to get out. He just let out one of his "EEE" sounds as I lowered the ladder into the basement.

I began reflecting about the kinds of predicaments I have gotten myself into because I hadn't thought fully enough. I realized that I am not all that different from Patrick. Too many times I have opted for what I thought would feel good at the time or satisfy an immediate need. Too often I have given in to the temptation to sin. It was simple enough to get Patrick out of the basement, but when it comes to my own sins, that is another story. In reality what I need to do is to allow God to make of me what He wills, and this is very hard for me. I need to be more willing to ask God what He wants of me instead of doing what I want. I need to allow Him to be the potter to my clay and to mold me in His image. And so again I pray, "Mold me and make me, Lord. Mold me and make me."

"For who has known the mind of the Lord, or who has been his counselor? Or who has given a gift to him that he might be repaid? For from him and through him and to him are all things. To him be glory forever. Amen."

Romans 11:34-36

Chapter Three

Missionaries for Christ

April 2, 2001

My Dear Patrick,

We talked to Sean in Center Harbor today. School is going very well for him. Daddy and I will be going to visit him next month. We want to be there for his Confirmation. Even though he has much going on there at school, his main concern was for you. He wanted to know all about your visit home for spring break and how you did returning to school. Sean loves you very much, and it is hard for him to be away from you and not be able to take care of you. For many years Sean followed you around the house and the yard making sure you didn't get hurt. Now, while he is away, he prays for you every day.

I know it must be hard for you to be back at Silvercrest. When you left to come home for spring break all the staff there thought you would not be coming back. They cleaned out your room and sent all your things with us. Daddy didn't say a word. He just picked up all your things and loaded them into the car. We knew you would be back, but you didn't seem to understand when we explained to you that you were only coming home for a week.

Your attorney advised us to take you back even though Silvercrest said your time had expired. As hard as it was to do, we knew it was best. Patrick, it is not safe for you to be at home. It was a very difficult week. It seemed as though with each day the situation got worse, to the point where you were in almost constant danger of hurting yourself or someone else. For days we worried and wondered what might happen when you returned to school. If they didn't take you back, I worried that the confusion would be very hard on you.

You were so upset when we turned on to highway 50, the road from Loogootee that leads to Silvercrest. It was such a difficult trip to make, especially when we didn't know what to expect. When we arrived, all our worries about them not accepting you were put to rest. The staff was surprised to see you, but they welcomed you with open arms and helped you put your things away.

You didn't seem happy or sad, just indifferent to the whole situation. I looked at your beautiful face and knew that there had to be so many questions, so many things you wanted to say, and yet there was no way to say them. Someday Patrick you will be heard. Someday, with God's help, we will learn to listen and understand. God bless, you my little one.

I love you,
Mommy

"And He said to them, 'Go into all the world and preach the gospel to the whole of creation.'" Mark 16:15

I walked back into the living room after quickly putting away some laundry. Patrick was jumping on the couch, covered in mud, with an open jar of peanut butter in his hands. I could not tell what was mud and what was peanut butter. My firm rules about not eating in the living room or jumping on the couch—especially in muddy shoes—and coming in covered in mud, did not seem to have sunk in very well. Patrick can hear a bag of potato chips opening from three rooms away, but he can't seem to follow any of the rules around the house. He simply acts as if he has never known that jumping on the couch, covered in mud, while eating peanut butter is not allowed.

It hadn't rained in a very long time, so I could not imagine where the mud had come from. A quick glance outside was all it took to figure out that someone had turned the hose on, possibly to wash one of the many bikes left lying in the yard. In a prayerful mumble I said, "Doesn't anyone around here understand a single word I'm saying? Lord, I feel like I'm in a foreign land where the natives don't speak my language, follow my customs, or even care what I'm trying to teach them." At that moment the Gospel of Matthew, chapter 28 verses 19 and 20 came to mind: These verses, known as The Great Commission, proclaim, "Go, therefore, and make disciples of all nations, baptizing them in the name of the Father and of the Son and of the Holy Spirit, teaching them to observe all that I have commanded you; and lo, I am with you always, to the close of the age."

Before I had time to say, "OK, Lord, I'm ready. What land do you want me to go to? What people do you want me to teach the faith to? Send me out. Now would be a good time." I heard in my heart, "You are there. Start at home, and teach my children." I had to pause for a moment to let it sink in. In that moment of silence it became clear that God was not asking me at that point to go out like the apostles and convert a pagan planet to Christianity. Instead, He wants me to bring His love to my children, to form them and teach them to obey His commands, and yet it seems the harder I try, the less they obey.

One night my three-year-old Emily would not go to sleep. She had not had a nap, and I thought she would collapse in exhaustion. At eleven o'clock, after several sips of water and trips to the bathroom, I peeked in her room and thought she was sound asleep. By this time, I was exhausted, and I went to bed. A few minutes later I heard her walking into my room. As she reached the head of the bed I saw in her hand a pen, with a book and piece of paper tucked under her arm. She looked at me and in a serious little voice and said, "Mom…" She paused and took a deep breath. "I need you to show me what to do for my school work." The lessons I wanted to teach her at that moment were how to tell time and what the words "stay in bed" mean. I think we will be working on those for quite a while yet, but even more importantly, I needed to take the opportunity to teach her about the love, patience, and forgiveness of Christ. I think it is a lesson easier to preach, than to teach, especially to a three-year-old late at night.

It's very frustrating when no matter what I say or what I do, I just can't get through to my children. They act like they understand me. I usually even get a "Yes, Mom" from them. I don't know if I've just taught them to say "Yes, Mom" when I'm talking to them, or if they really understand what I'm saying. The frustration of not being understood is an all day long trial for Patrick. No matter how hard he tries, often we can't figure out what he wants. It is not unusual for Patrick to come to us with his hand out crying. We ask him over and over again, "What do you want?" Usually, by the time he asks for something he is so upset that he can't use pictures or signs although some times he will try to say parts of words. The trouble is that it's so hard to figure out what those words are between all the squeals and sobs.

At age ten Patrick's irritation at not being understood became so great that he began to hit in frustration. At first it was occasional, and we would just hold him and try to calm him down. It upset us when he would hit, not so much because it would hurt, because it usually didn't, but because we knew that eventually it would. We were right. In the past few years, Patrick's frustration has increased. Sometimes he tolerates not being understood very well, and at other times he hits very hard, kicks, and even has started to bite himself and others. It breaks my heart to see him so upset.

Patrick doesn't seem to understand what to do when he can't make himself understood, or when things don't go quite the way he wants them. I do. I frequently think of saints, like Mother Cabrini. She came to the United States from Italy to work with immigrants and to teach them. Not only was she in a foreign land, but also she was working with children who themselves were many times orphans living in a foreign land. The language barrier must have been great, and yet she did not always need words to teach them what she most wanted them to know: the love of Christ.

Each time I'm tempted to say, "How many times do I have to tell you... or I've told you a million times," I catch myself because I know that God could be saying exactly the same thing to me. I know my children will struggle with sins of laziness, disobedience, and many others throughout their lives, just as I do. As important as it is for my children to learn obedience, I want them to obey, to avoid sin out of love for Christ and not just to avoid one of my lectures every time I step on a toy or trip over their shoes. Like Patrick, I will have days when no one seems to hear a single word I say, yet I need to be willing even on those days to go out and make disciples of all nations starting with my family in the nation we call home.

"But Jesus said, 'Let the children come to me, and do not hinder them; for to such belongs the kingdom of heaven.'"
Matthew 19:14

CHAPTER FOUR

Duct Tape?

May 21, 2001

Dear Patrick,

May has been a wonderful month, Patrick. The weather has been so nice, and you've been in a good mood each time we've visited. I guess the nice weather makes us all a little more cheerful. I want to tell you about so much that has gone on this month so that none of us forget. We came home from New Hampshire a couple weeks ago. It was great to see Sean at his school. It was Parents' Weekend, and he was getting confirmed with the rest of his class. Mommy and I were very fortunate to be able to fly out to be with him. Uncle Greg and Aunt Elizabeth came from North Carolina, too. Uncle Greg was Sean's confirmation sponsor. It was a great time. We stayed in a beautiful bed and breakfast that overlooked Red Hill just outside Center Harbor. Around here we would call Red Hill a mountain! It was a gorgeous place, and we enjoyed our trip greatly.

Patrick, we spent a lot of time talking about you to Uncle Greg and Aunt Elizabeth. Everyone is always so interested to hear how you are doing. Finally, I think we have some great news! You are going to be able to stay at Silvercrest until we can get you placed in a new school. The staff there has been so nice to us and to you recently. Even though we have had the pressure of the lawsuit, they are really keeping your best interests in mind. We appreciate that so much.

We held a case conference for you recently, and everyone seems to think that we have a good plan now. Your advocate is really good at what she does. She has encouraged us to begin looking at state-of-the art schools even if they are out of Indiana. In fact, she has placed several boys and girls at schools all across the country. I didn't even know it was an option, Patrick. I know it sounds crazy to send you somewhere even farther away, but it just may help to get you back home more quickly. You see, so many of these schools spe-

cialize in helping children just like you who have communication and aggression problems. They are doing such wonderful work with special children. Mommy and I have started looking on the Internet to research possible schools for you to attend. The bad news is that the best ones we have found are in Massachusetts, Florida, Pennsylvania, and Kansas. The good news is that we are going to find the one that works best for you and will help you learn as fast as possible how to deal with your problems.

The other good news, Patrick, is that Mommy is going to publish her book about you. I think it is great that people will be able to read your story and the way that you have blessed our lives! Isn't God awesome? Here you are, a boy who can't even speak, and yet God has worked through your mom to tell your story. I am so proud of your mommy, Patrick, and I'm proud of you too for working as hard as you can to learn and to get better. I know it must be hard for you to be away from us, and I know it's hard for you to keep struggling through all your problems. I know you don't realize it, but I struggle too, Patrick. Yes, my struggles are different from yours, and you may never understand them. It is so hard to have one of my children away from me. I could never have conceived the love I would feel for each of you before all of you were born. It helps me through my struggles to know that, as much as I love you and your brothers and sisters, God loves me even more. And that is a story I need to tell.

I love you, Patrick.
Daddy

"He is before all things, and in him all things hold together."
Colossians 1:17

Duct tape. Duct tape has to be among the greatest of all inventions. What household can be without it? I know it has become cliché that one can fix anything with duct tape, but it is very nearly true. I began looking around my house to count all the things I've used duct tape to fix. I found the following: a cabinet panel where a mirror used to be, (Michael broke it.) the bottom vent on our refrigerator, (fallen off again.) various pieces of heating ducts, the face plate on a kitchen drawer, a holy water font, a piece of molding in the boys' room, a severed baby doll head, the hinge on a toy chest, and various items in the garage. The tape has worked amazingly well in most instances, but it is usually not a total fix but simply a stopgap measure.

One item in our house that I haven't been able to use duct tape to fix is our dining room table. The table is over 100 years old. Beth's aunt Sister Maria Tasto found it for us in the basement of her Benedictine monastery in Ferdinand, Indiana. We believe it was used for a sewing table for the Sisters in times past because there are two drawers on either side where fabric and sewing supplies would fit nicely. The table measures nine and a half feet in length and is a deep maple color. Three large planks make up its top, and it sways slightly in the middle. It's not exactly a museum piece, but we love it.

We couldn't find matching chairs, so we pieced together a set of twelve chairs bought at an auction from the old Cathedral High School library in Indianapolis and discarded dining room chairs from Sister Maria's convent. A wonderful older man whom we had befriended added three inches to the table legs in his workshop so the chairs would fit underneath. The first time our neighbor from across the street saw the table he commented, "Wow! Where's Jesus?" It would have been a tight fit for Jesus and His disciples, but you get the picture.

This table has been the centerpiece of our home for the past ten years. It has been the scene of countless breakfasts, lunches, and dinners. It has served as the venue for family prayer and discussion. It has been command central for Cub Scout and Brownie crafts, science projects, retreat planning meetings, All Saints' Day costume designing, Christmas card writing, bill paying, and even the occasional diaper changing. In recent years, it has become the center of our home school classroom. Years from now I suspect it will be one of the things that come to the minds of our children when they think of home.

Over the years Patrick and the other children have given the table even more character. Patrick used to pound his fork into it when he was upset during meals. Some of the other younger children picked up on his habit, and so the table is now pock marked in places. We also have a few areas where wood filler has chipped away. These places are perfect for collecting crumbs of toast, bits of cereal, and fragments of potato chips. For those areas, we use the vacuum cleaner hose to clean up. Ours is not the kind of dining room table that lies waiting in a formal dining area for Thanksgiving and Christmas feasts. No, this classic table is an integral part of our daily lives.

I have seen some parents panic when children damage their furniture or appliances. I don't necessarily like it when Patrick uses the couch or bed for a trampoline, or when one of the other kids decides to enliven our walls with colored markers and crayons. Beth and I decided early on in our marriage, however, that everything we owned was subject to immediate and sometimes permanent alteration, and we weren't going to let it upset us. It simply isn't worth having if we are going to get so upset. Our ten children haven't always shared our desire to keep the house and its contents in working order. I am constantly trying to repair broken chairs, end tables, ice makers, cabinet drawers, pieces of molding, kitchen faucets, bathroom drains, stuck windows, and faulty light bulbs. Notice I say trying to repair. I am sometimes successful, but it is rarely permanent. I think there is a direct correlation between the amount of pride I feel at accomplishing a task and the likelihood that I will be repeating the same task in a matter of days or weeks. Beth has always been someone who likes to keep "To Do" lists. A short time into our child rearing years I grew to dislike these lists a great deal. Beth used to talk about the feeling of accomplishment that came with striking a big line through the tasks as they were completed, but I never have been able to get to the end of the list before I have to start all over again. My rudimentary handyman skills have never been able to compete with the nearly endless list of repairs and upgrades. Now that we use our computer daily, crashing systems, lost files, malfunctioning software, and broken printers have found their way onto my list as well.

When it all comes down to it, all of these things are just that—things. I have come to realize over the years that I am never going to be able to fix everything that needs to be fixed or to paint everything that needs to be painted. Don't get me wrong. I try to stay on top of these household tasks, but far more important than the state of our house is the state of our souls: Beth's, the children's, and mine. If I get everything in perfect working order and create a showplace home, it's not going to matter much in the long run. Yes, it is important to complete the tasks that God puts before me, but I have to remember which is the most important task.

The most important task God has given me is the responsibility to provide for the spiritual well being of my wife and children. All else must be and is secondary. A piece of duct tape is not going to fix a broken relationship, and it isn't going to heal a spiritual ailment. For that I must employ the super power of God's grace. Jesus reminds us in Matthew 6:20 that "where your treasure is, there will your heart be also." If I am seeking earthly treasure, my heart will surely follow. If I am seeking the treasure of heaven for my family and for me, that too will help to dictate my actions. My "To Do" list must say, "Pray. Read Scripture. Go to Mass. Receive the Sacraments. Love your wife and children. Serve others." God's grace is the ultimate in spiritual duct tape. Not only does it work to fix up what is wrong with us, but also—unlike my repairs—it offers permanent forgiveness, permanent reparation, and permanent salvation. This is our hope. And this is our faith.

"Blessed are the poor in spirit, for theirs is the kingdom of heaven."

Matthew 5:3

Chapter Five

Helping Hand

June 25, 2001

My Dear Patrick,

We have some exciting news for you. God has blessed you with another baby brother or sister. The baby will be born in January, just after Christmas. Michael is hoping and praying it is a boy. I think he is tired of being the baby boy around the house, and he has waited many years for a little brother. I remember how excited Sean and Laura were when we brought you home from the hospital. They could hardly keep their hands off you. It was a good thing you liked to be held. Very rarely did you cry; it always seemed like you were smiling. It didn't take much for Sean or Laura to get you to laugh. Maybe someday you will be able to hold and play with this special little baby. God has surrounded you with so many wonderful brothers and sisters who love you very much.

God is always blessing us. Many times it is in ways we never could have imagined. We are continuing our search for the perfect school for you. I would never have dreamed that all this was possible. The thought that we could ever send you to one of the best schools in the country never entered my head. Now we only need to decide which one would be best. Having you far away from us is still very hard, but if it is what it will take to bring you back home, we will do it.

Your advocate and our local school are working hard to get all the paper work together. It has required many meetings for Daddy and me, but we don't mind. The hard part is when we sit through these meetings only to have our concerns ignored, or to be totally misunderstood. I'm sure you know what that is like. It is very painful to talk about sending you away, because that is far from what we wanted for you. I know everyone is trying to help, but at times we get the feeling that they have totally forgotten that it is the life of our precious son we are talking about.

Once the packets of information are put together, they will be sent out to the schools that we have chosen. At that point, each school will begin to look and see if it has the right place for you. This will all take quite a while. Until then you will need to stay at the school you are at now. I wish I could come and see you right now. Patrick, I want to hug you and tell you that everything will be all right, but I can't. God has always provided everything you need. He will not stop now. What we need to do is be patient and pray for Him to guide us. I miss you so much. God bless you, my little one.

I love you,
Mommy

"And my God will supply every need of yours according to his riches in glory in Christ Jesus."

Philippians 4:19

Mark and I made our way through the streets of our small town. It was a rare chance to be alone; we were out on a date. It wasn't the kind of date you might have imagined. Let's just say we had big plans. It was just before eight when we headed out the door. The kids were fed and ready for bed. Patrick was hopping around the living room watching one of his favorite movies. I thought I had taken care of all the minute details. You can imagine my surprise when we pulled up in front of the laundromat and read the sign CLOSED. It closed at eight. How could I have forgotten to call and check their hours? Our plans were ruined.

With ten loads of dirty laundry in the back of our van, we headed home. Within moments we came upon a friend's house where some men from our church were meeting for prayer. Mark was supposed to be at the meeting but felt like our big plans were more important at the time. God had other plans as usual. I told Mark to go ahead to the meeting, and I would take the unwashed laundry home.

Our washer had broken a few days before for the third time in as many months. I had left messages with the repairman but had not heard back from him. I assumed he was out of town or simply too busy to respond. The laundry was piling up quickly, and despite his best efforts, Mark couldn't figure out what was wrong with the machine. Patrick's bedding alone can be two loads a day. If you add to that the towels from frequent baths you have a few more loads, and that doesn't even include the rest of the family's clothes and towels. Patrick had mastered the art of creating laundry at a very young age.

The next morning the repairman showed up to work on the washer. After apologizing for the delay, he disappeared into the laundry room. Within a few minutes the phone rang. It was one of Mark's friends from the prayer meeting. Mark must have mentioned our canceled date the night before, because his friend said that a new washer was being delivered to our home in the afternoon and wanted to know if that was O.K. Somewhat in shock, and yet very grateful, I said, "Yes." I knew there was no way we could afford a new washer, and I had been praying hard that we simply could afford to get the old one fixed one more time. Just as I hung up the phone our repairman emerged from the laundry room and said, "I've got some bad news. It's going to cost a lot to fix it this time, and I don't know how long it will last. I think you would be much better off just getting a new washer." I was able to smile and say, "O.K." God was way ahead of us in providing for our needs.

A year later while driving to Silvercrest to visit with Patrick I found myself worrying and wondering. I was filled with worries about how we would provide for Patrick. At the same time I was wondering if we had become a burden to our family and friends. Even though we almost never asked for help, help was always being offered in one way or another. I try never to turn away offers for help because I believe they come from the hand of God. On this day, I worried. I worried about how much our family and friends may have had to go out of their way, and what sort of trouble we may have caused them.

As we pulled up in front of his school, I tried to forget my concerns and focus on the beautiful day and the fact that we would be spending it with Patrick. As usual we started our visit with one of Patrick's favorite things. We went out for pizza. For some reason, as crowded as the restaurant was when we came in, a lady at the table next to ours noticed us. I guess it's hard not to be noticed with our troupe of kids. She asked many of the same questions I have heard many times, and love to answer, like, "Are these all yours?" and "What is autism?" Patrick was having one of his moments when the anticipation of pizza makes him jump up and down in his chair, squeal with delight, and flap his hands. A short while later, she asked me a question I had not heard before. She said, "I always wanted many children, and God gave me three that I am very grateful for. He has blessed us with very much." She then went on to ask, with tears in her eyes, "Would you let me do something?" I said yes. She put her hand in mine, and then quickly walked out of the restaurant. In my hand she had left a fifty-dollar bill, but even more she had left the answer to my worries and concerns.

Last November I received a rather large amount of money in a birthday card from a relative. I was somewhat shocked when I opened the card, not sure what the money was for. That night our furnace broke down, and we awakened in the morning to a very cold house. We did not need a new furnace, but by the time the old one was repaired it cost close to what I received in the birthday card the night before.

The money is not always there before we need it, however. A friend of mine once told me that whenever it looks like there's not enough money to pay the bills, she starts writing some checks for God. They always have had enough. There have been many times when we had to wait, wonder, and pray. God does not always provide in the way we had hoped, or at the time we think best, but He always provides. Then in His goodness He uses what we no longer need to provide for others.

St. Basil the Great said, "The bread you store up belongs to the hungry; the cloak that lies in your chest belongs to the naked; the gold you have hidden in the ground belongs to the poor." And who are these hungry, naked, and poor? They are Christ. Everything belongs to Him. Time and again God has shown me that it does not matter if we are rich or poor. What matters is that we love Him and trust Him enough to receive, to receive in all humility, and then to freely give it all back, without worry or concern.

"Jesus said to him, 'If you would be perfect, go, sell what you possess and give to the poor, and you will have treasure in heaven; and come, follow Me.'"

Matthew 19:21

Chapter Six

Slow Down, You Run Too Fast

August 24, 2001

Dear Patrick,

I have to tell you about our trip to Wichita. I am so excited because I know that we have found a perfect school for you. It's been such a confusing summer with all the meetings, all the questions about your future, and all the research into schools, but I think this is the one. Heartspring is such a wonderful place, Patrick, and you will fit in perfectly there.

Mommy and I traveled out to Kansas with two ladies from the special education co-op. Mom was complaining about the trip because the pregnancy is already causing her a lot of problems. We had to go from home to Evansville, to Cincinnati, to Kansas City, and then on to Wichita. She started complaining but heard the Lord say, "Would you rather go by donkey?" That put it all in perspective. I've been looking forward to this trip ever since we learned that they have a possible spot for you. We had to fly to Kansas City, and then drive nearly four hours to Wichita. It was a nice drive though, because the ladies with us are really nice people. We had a lot to discuss, and I know they want what is best for you.

It was really hot in Wichita, about 105 degrees. The heat has never seemed to bother you much, so I don't think you would have minded. We met with the director of admissions, Charles, and he took us out to dinner at a nice Italian restaurant. We hit it off really well with Charles, and he told us all about the school. It turns out that it is the same place your great uncle, Father John Tasto, attended when he was studying for the priesthood. Isn't that a neat coincidence? He was having difficulty with stuttering, so they sent him to Heartspring. Now, he preaches to thousands with no trouble and has even given retreats to the Missionaries of Charity. The school has changed a lot since then, and now they work almost exclusively with autistic children like you.

All the staff had seen the video we sent them of you from Silvercrest, and they had reviewed all your records. They believe you will fit in there, Patrick, and so do I. The boys live in group homes with eight children each. They help with the daily chores and live together like a family. I know it isn't like living at home, and I hate how far away it is, but I think you will like it. There is even a YMCA nearby where you can swim. We're hoping to be able to send you there just long enough to teach you all you need to know to live back home. I don't know how long that will take.

I'm sure this doesn't make sense to you now, but I pray that it will one day. Mommy and I want nothing more than for you to be back at home. It's where you belong, but it isn't what is best for you now. Can you possibly understand that? There are so many things you have to learn. Heartspring can help you get there.

I'm really glad that Mommy encouraged me to write to you. It helps me focus on the things I want to tell you someday. I keep praying that one day you will be able to sit down and read the letters, or that I can read them to you and you'll understand. School has been in session for a couple weeks now. As I was getting ready for school this year, I couldn't help but think of you and wonder what this next year of school will be like for you. Now that you are twelve, you will be in seventh grade. I have loved working with seventh graders ever since I was in college and lived at the Outpost, our diocesan youth camp.

Patrick, I thought you would be in a different school by now, but you're still at Silvercrest waiting to go to Kansas. I wonder if you are as confused as I am about the future. It's probably better that God has chosen not to reveal the future to us, or we would be too scared to go on at times. I'll just keep praying and hoping that everything becomes clear soon. Until then, little buddy, I'll be thinking about you and praying for you as you get ready for your seventh grade year. I'm sure it will be very different for you. I have so much hope. We'll be down to see you this weekend. I can't wait to play with you on the swings and take you out for pizza. Until then, know that I keep you in my daily thoughts and prayers.

I love you,
Daddy

"Be still and know that I am God. I am exalted among the nations, I am exalted in the earth!"
Psalm 46:10

I had been looking forward to the trip for months. As much as I hate to be away from Beth and the kids, this was an opportunity that simply was too good to pass up. In the summer of 2001, I was one of 15 teachers from across the United States and Canada invited to travel to Harvard to take part in a Liberty Fund colloquium entitled, "Teachers in a Free Society." The other teachers and I had prepared for several weeks by reading Socrates, Plato, Aristotle, Horace Mann, and John Locke. We also studied more modern novels such as *Goodbye, Mr. Chips* and *The Prime of Miss Jean Brodie*. Our task was to study the history and development of teaching in the United States and to try to determine what role we teachers play in our society. We stayed off-campus at a bed and breakfast built in the 1700's that had once been the home of Henry David Thoreau. As an English teacher who loves United States history, the combination of reading, collegiality, and setting was absolutely wonderful.

I flew to Boston on a Friday in July and met our oldest son, Sean, at Logan Airport. He was flying from Boston back to Indiana, and we had about an hour together in a most interesting but unexpected environment. Two months later terrorists left from the very terminal we met in to fly into the World Trade Center. Sean was heading home for a two-week break from his school, Immaculate Conception Apostolic School in New Hampshire. Fortunately, I was to be gone for one week only, so we would have some time together at home. It was a strange feeling to see my then nearly fifteen-year-old son for the first time in several months at an airport 1200 miles from home. I was happy to know, however, that he was trying to follow God's will for his life. Beth often commented that, as hard as it was to allow Sean to leave for school, it was like sending him off to an amusement park; whereas, sending Patrick off to his residential school was much more like a prison sentence.

The sessions at Harvard were going great for the first day and a half. We were engaged in high-level discussions with classmates and were excited by what we were accomplishing. It was all I could do intellectually to keep up with this group of teachers, but the challenge was exhilarating. That Saturday evening I called Beth to share my excitement and to say hi to the kids. I always phone home with a certain amount of trepidation because I'm never too sure what kinds of tricks Patrick may have had up his sleeve. This day was no different as Beth related the following story:

Beth and the kids had been getting ready to go to my niece, Amber's, wedding. Beth was taking everything in stride even though most mothers would panic at the mere thought of getting eight children ready for a wedding without her husband around. (The plan was for Patrick to stay at home with some dear, saintly friends, Pat and Amy.) Beth was doing great, especially for a mother in the first trimester of her tenth pregnancy dealing with the accompanying nausea and fatigue. She was dressing the little girls when Patrick pointed to the door wanting to go out to swing. Beth said, "Quick, Brendan. Put your shoes on and go out with Patrick." Somehow in the few seconds it took for Brendan to get outside, our 12-year old Houdini had vanished.

Brendan came back in to say that he couldn't find Patrick, so Beth sent him back out to head toward the neighbor's pool. She sent a few of the other kids to look in the backyard while she searched the house to see if he had somehow come back in. It was no use. Patrick had vanished. Sean headed out into the woods to follow the creek, but he turned back a few minutes later because he couldn't make it through the thick underbrush. After about a half hour of driving through the neighborhood, searching pools, the creek, and the woods, Beth called my parents and other relatives and friends to start looking for Patrick even though most of them were dressed for the wedding too.

A couple driving down a country road about two miles from our house found Patrick. They didn't recognize him, but their son, Jordan, one of my students, did. Jordan drove to our house to tell Beth that his parents had found our son. By that time our friends, Pat and Amy, had arrived to join in the search. They headed off to pick him up. Patrick was walking on the side of a freshly blacktopped road covered in tar. He was barefoot and shirtless, a mere fifty yards from a busy state highway. Patrick's guardian angels were busily working overtime as he continued to run his solitary race to God knows where.

Why was Patrick running? What was he trying to find? Where was he going? I have no idea. My heart sank as Beth related the story to me across the miles. I had just had a fabulous day at Harvard and now felt so guilty for being gone. I was so eager to share it all with Beth, and, suddenly, I wanted to be nowhere but home. My role as father to Patrick and our other nine children is of greatest importance to me. I'm sure it doesn't always look that way to an outsider. It's very difficult to balance the busy work schedule that my job dictates with the vocation of being a husband and father. In addition to teaching English classes, I am the director of our school-to-work program and coach academic teams and athletic teams. In short, I am very busy. I suspect though that I'm no different from most fathers who struggle to balance their careers with their home lives. Our days begin early, end late, and are filled with one thing or another every moment in between. It is so hard to strike the balance between work and home and to remember always what should come first. It is not uncommon for men to derive their sense of self-esteem from their work, and that makes it even more difficult.

We're all busy trying to accomplish what God has set before us. Quite often during the busyness of my day, I will say a short prayer to the Holy Spirit for inspiration. "Holy Spirit, please guide me. Give me the words to say in this meeting," or "Give me the words this parent needs to hear." It is so hard for me to slow down for long enough to even do that. Too often I hurry through the appointments of each day barely recognizing the presence of God. When I do take the time to pause and to reflect, I realize that I often have very little control over what goes on each day. I am desperately in need of God's Grace. I know that I cannot accomplish the tasks that God has set before me without the Grace that flows through His Sacraments and through prayer.

I got off the phone and thanked God for my wonderful wife who was "holding down the fort." I also thanked Him that our bed and breakfast was just a half block away from a Catholic church. That morning I had awakened early and gone to 7:00

A.M. Mass before our sessions started and had sneaked away for Confession during the afternoon break. The grace from those sacraments would see me through until I could make it home again. I also felt that somehow God was taking that grace and sharing it with my family until I could be with them again. What an awesome God!

"Every athlete exercises self-control in all things. They do it to receive a perishable wreath, but we an imperishable. Well, I do not run aimlessly, I do not box as one beating the air; but I pummel my body and subdue it, lest after preaching to others I myself should be disqualified."

1 Corinthians 9:25-27

Chapter Seven

Stop Playing

September 8, 2001

My Dear Patrick,

We have missed you so much. As each day passes, it is harder and harder to be away from you. You are so precious to us, and yet it seems as though our entire focus has become sending you away. Daddy and I are willing to do whatever God wants, even if it means you have to leave us for a while.

We thought we would be taking you to a wonderful school in Kansas. We have spent weeks planning and setting everything up. As hard as it was to think of you so far away, we felt that it was best so that you can one day move back home. Patrick, you need a lot of help to get well, and the school seems to offer a great deal of hope.

Tomorrow morning Daddy and I were scheduled to fly with you to Kansas. Our return flight was scheduled for the afternoon of September 11. We waited for weeks for one last thing, the final approval from the state department of education. It seemed to only be a matter of paper work. As the day for us to leave drew nearer, we began to wonder if you would ever be going. Daddy wrote to our Congressmen and contacted a few other people he thought might be able to help us get an answer. We did not hear from any of them.

A letter arrived yesterday afternoon. The state rejected your placement at the school. The letter said that if we had any questions we should feel free to call. I called because the reasons for rejection made no sense to me. When I called, however, they told me they could not talk to me, and I would have to talk to my lawyer. That means you will not be able to go to school there unless we take more legal action. There has been so much confusion in our minds. We thought that your going to the school was the answer to all our prayers. And now we discover you may not be able to go.

This morning we got up early to take the family to a conference in Lexington, Kentucky called Reclaim the Flame. We didn't think we would be going this year because there were still so many last minute things to do to get ready for our trip to Kansas. After finding out you could not go, we told your brothers and sisters we would go ahead to the conference.

I sat down at the table where your little sister, Bridget, was sitting alone eating breakfast. My mind was racing with questions. I was asking God over and over again for answers, answers to all the many questions that were tearing my heart apart. Bridget suddenly stopped eating her cereal and began to sing. She sang part of a song from the movie Joseph, King of Dreams. It comes from a part of the movie when Joseph is in prison in Egypt after having been sold into slavery by his brothers and then falsely accused of a crime. The song is his prayer to God.

She may not have had the words exactly right, but this is what she sang. "You know better than I. You know the way, and I'll let go the need to know why. I'll take what answers you provide, 'cause you know better than I." Then she went back to eating her Cheerios without another word. I can't say how much that song meant to me at that moment. We can see God's plan for Joseph was to save his family and all of Egypt from famine and drought. I don't know what God has in store for you, and I guess at this time I don't need to know.

Tomorrow we won't be going to Kansas, and that is O.K. In time God will surely show us what to do. For now we continue to pray and sing along with Bridget. God bless you, my little one.

I love you,
Mommy

"For I know the plans I have for you, plans to prosper, not to harm you."
Jeremiah 29:11

The kids were dressed and ready to go. It was time to get into the van for a two and a half hour drive to Indianapolis. Most of the family at least acted like they knew the plan. There are always a few of the children who seem quite startled when I say it's time to get in the van. After giving me a look of confusion, as though I could not possibly be talking to them, they proceed to list all the things that must be done before they could ever consider leaving the house.

Today was no exception. Our plan was to go to the hospital in Indianapolis to visit Grandpa, who was recovering from surgery. From there we planned to head to the Indianapolis Children's Museum for the afternoon. When everything was done, lost shoes found, and precious toys in hand, we started getting everyone into the van. I had sent Patrick out first, and now we could not find him. This was not unusual, but I had just gotten him dressed in a nice clean outfit. He even had his shoes and socks on, a rarity. It had only been a few minutes since I told him to get in the van. I told him where we were going and why. I knew he would love the Children's Museum. Obviously, he wasn't interested, or perhaps he didn't understand. In either case, he had other plans.

I hesitated before sending anyone out to look for him. I had to choose my helpers wisely, or I could end up with not one, but many missing children, with even more missing shoes, and even more dirty clothes. I opted to look for Patrick myself. I went into the backyard and looked down to the creek. Sure enough, there was Patrick, clothes and shoes off, happily splashing in the water. After calling his name several times, he finally looked at me, more like a pest that would not go away, than as his mother calling him to come along on a wonderful trip to a place full of more fun than he could imagine.

When my efforts failed, and I could not coax him up from the creek, Mark took over. He made his way down the steep hill, through the trees and heavy brush, to the creek. It's not easy to get down to our creek unless you happen to be Patrick. He can make it down in what seems like a split second. When Mark finally captured him and started leading him up the hill, Patrick was not very happy, but he gave in and followed along. I'm sure it made a lot more sense to him to play in the creek than to sit in the hot van for hours. The fact that the Children's Museum, complete with carousel rides, would be at the end of the journey didn't seem to matter to him. He knew what he wanted, and he wasn't happy about his plans being changed.

Long drives are often difficult for Patrick. We are not sure what exactly bothers him. We can only go by trial and error plus any information from adult autistics who can talk and share their experiences. What we do know is that many things irritate him, like loud, high-pitched noises. There is no way to predict for sure when a two-year-old girl will scream, especially while traveling in a van down the highway. What we were asking Patrick to do was to stop doing something that seemed so right, and so comforting to him, and instead to do something that would be very hard, and probably very painful. I'm sure it made no sense to him, and yet he gave in and got into the van not knowing what was in store for him.

I have to ask myself, "Would I have done the same?" Day by day, hour by hour, minute by minute, I struggle with small irritations. They usually come in the form of spilled juice, minor disobediences, financial concerns, flu season, or my need for a clean, orderly house. In between the small day-to-day struggles, there have been great trials to bear, pain and suffering that change things from the way I had planned for them to go. Is this any different than Patrick getting in the van? I don't think so. Through baptism I became a child of God, and if I truly believe that, then I should be able to trust in His plan for me. Even if it includes painful trials I can't understand.

Yesterday my son Brendan brought me the baby, Connor, when he began to cry. He had been a little fussy, but now he was very upset. It was bedtime, and he wanted to nurse. I also knew that he was teething, so he needed something to ease the pain of his gums, and also he needed a diaper change. None of my plans made him happy. My plans were to give him some medicine to ease the pain, to change his diaper to prevent diaper rash, and to put him in his warm sleeper so he wouldn't get cold during the night. He only screamed more loudly and kicked making it much harder to get him ready for bed. I knew that nursing had to come last because it would put him to sleep, but there was no way to explain all of this to a baby. He had to wait for what must have seemed like a long time, but, in the end, he was comfortable, warm, well fed, and sound asleep.

This great struggle for Patrick and myself to accept what we don't understand reminds me of a story I once heard. There was once a horrible fire that quickly consumed the downstairs of a family's home. The father knew his young son was upstairs in his room, and he wanted desperately to go in and rescue his young son, but there was no way. He would have died in the fire. The father could see his son through the smoke standing in the window crying out, "Daddy, help me! It hurts" The father and the firemen quickly held out a net to catch the child. The father then called to his son, "Jump, we will catch you." The little boy yelled back, "I can't jump, Daddy. I can't see you." The father responded, "I know you can't, but I can see you, Son. Now jump!" The boy jumped into the net, and into the loving arms of his father.

In the end, Patrick and Connor had no choice but to go along with my plans. Ready or not, they were going to have to do what I wanted. Connor screamed to the very end. Patrick eventually gave up what he wanted to do and reluctantly got into the van. Daily, in my morning offering, I give my entire day and myself to God. I want to rest secure in his arms as a child being cared for by a loving Parent. Like Patrick, I need to be willing to stop what I want to do, what seems the best to me, and to go along with my Father on a noisy, bumpy ride, knowing He is taking me somewhere greater and more wonderful than I could ever imagine.

"I consider that the sufferings of this present time are not worth comparing to the glory that is to be revealed to us."

Romans 8:18

Chapter Eight

Let's Face It

October 25, 2001

Dear Patrick,

I'm on fall break, and I've been painting the living room. Even though it's late October, the weather has been really beautiful. I wanted to take a break to write to you about all the crazy things that have been going on. We'll be down to visit you at Silvercrest again tomorrow. I can't believe you are still there, but you will be coming home soon.

After we got the rejection letter from the state I had a huge decision to make. I had been praying so hard for guidance trying to decide what to do. I called your attorney to talk it over. It was a strange conversation. He really wanted us to go ahead with the lawsuit, and I didn't know what was best. I don't want to go into the details with you because you wouldn't understand, but we were actually going to win the case for you to go to Heartspring. The only problem was that we weren't going to win against the state but against our local school district, my employer. The attorney has had many similar cases in the past, and he was confident that this would be the outcome. As badly as I wanted you to go to Heartspring, and as much as I felt like that was the best thing for you, I just couldn't go on with the case. It would have hurt too many people, and we simply can't do that even if it is for a very good reason. When I told the attorney to drop the case he said, "If you drop the case you are an absolute fool." I told him I was just going to have to be a fool then. I hated to let him down because he had done so much for us over the past several months. It was not an easy thing to do. I felt really bad about the whole thing, but when I talked to Mommy about it and told her what the attorney said, she made me feel better. "There's your confirmation," she said. "God's ways are foolish to men." I guess you could say I was a fool for God.

We immediately began making plans for you to come home as difficult as that would be. I've been very happy knowing that you are coming home, but I'm still unsure about how things will work out. You're really not ready to come home, but we are going to try to do everything we can to help you. Your brothers and sisters are so happy to know you'll be home. They ask me every day, "How much longer is it until Patrick gets to come home?" I have to believe that God has an incredible plan in store for you, Patrick.

In the midst of all these new plans something else happened that we don't understand. You had a grand mal seizure. Do you remember anything about that? All the new tests and new doctors must add to your confusion. It certainly has made things more confusing for us. What is this new chapter in your life's story going to hold? Will you have more seizures or will this be the only one? As usual I don't have many answers for you. I'll just keep praying for you and will anxiously await the day you are home with us again.

I love you,
Dad

"Come now, you who say, 'Today or tomorrow we will go into such and such a town and spend a year there and trade and get gain'; whereas you do not know about tomorrow. What is your life? For you are a mist that appears for a little time and then vanishes. Instead you ought to say, 'If the Lord wills, we shall live and we shall do this or that.'"

James 4: 13-15

"Face it. You're going to lose." "Face it. Life's not fair." "Face it. You have to pay taxes." "Face it. You're not perfect." Benjamin Franklin is noted for saying, "There are only two certainties in life: death and taxes." I'm no philosopher, but I would add a third certainty: suffering. Throughout our lives we will all face times of difficulty, times when things just don't go our way. I've often heard people say that if everything is going o.k. just stick around, and it will change. It's kind of like our Midwestern weather. You never quite know what to expect.

Things are certainly like that with Patrick. Every time I think I know what treatment to use, what new medication to try, or what therapeutic device he needs, something will change. A new specialist will offer a different opinion or a friend will tell us about some new therapy. So little is known about how to treat children with autism. The medical community is researching and trying to learn all they can, but there is so much more they do not know. As parents we try to learn all we can too, but we are often faced with the realization of our own human limitations. One time when I thought we had a handle on where Patrick was heading and what we needed to do to help him best was just before he came home from Silvercrest, the developmental school he had been attending for nearly two years.

I was a team member on a Christ Renews His Parish retreat at St. Peter's, a nearby church, when a friend whispered a message to me. We had just come from spending time in prayer before the Blessed Sacrament when Chris pulled me aside and said, "Mark, you need to call home. Patrick had a grand mal seizure tonight." I immediately called Beth and found out what had happened. Patrick's nurse was administering his evening medication when the seizure occurred. That alone was a blessing, as she was rarely on duty at night. Patrick's eyes went back; he started a clicking sound; his face turned pale, and his lips became purple. Patrick then fell to the floor as his body shook. The nurse called for a code cart and administered oxygen. He fell asleep for about forty-five minutes when it was all over.

Upon hearing the news, I immediately left the retreat to be at home with Beth. As I drove home through the dark and cold late night my thoughts turned once again to Patrick. Was he upset by the seizure? Was he in any pain? Did he understand what was going on? It was so hard to think of Patrick lying there unconscious, unable to breathe, wearing an oxygen mask. I wanted so badly to be with him, but time and distance prohibited it. I went back to St. Peter's the next morning to let everyone know that Patrick was o.k. and to ask for prayers, and then Beth and I made the trip once more to the school in New Albany.

Seizure activity was completely new to us. We had heard that some autistic people begin experiencing seizures with adolescence, but there is no way to really prepare for something like that. Once again we were faced with new problems, new doctors, and new medication. As with all things, we really had no choice but to face it. Patrick underwent an EEG at a local hospital that proved inconclusive, so we weren't sure what had happened. We did know, however, that Patrick was coming home in a few weeks, and we were going to have to learn quickly what to do. We were simply going to have to face this new challenge. But how could we?

In situations like this, when we are faced with suffering or indecision of some sort, I find it helpful to look toward Jesus and His example. I was reflecting upon this when I recalled the story of Jesus in Luke 9. I have always found this chapter of Luke to be one of the most amazing accounts in the Gospel. So much goes on in this chapter. Jesus had instructed the Twelve about how to go out as preachers and gave them the authority to cast out demons and to heal diseases. He then preached in Bethsaida and fed five thousand men with five loaves and two fish. Next, Peter made his great confession and told Jesus that He was the Son of God, and Jesus responded by predicting His Passion.

Not long after that, Peter, James, and John accompanied Him to Mt. Tabor where they witnessed the Transfiguration of Jesus in His heavenly glory. Jesus came down from the mountain afterwards and cast out a demon, and all were astonished by His power. He then made a second prediction of His death and told the disciples that He would be delivered into the hands of men, but they still didn't understand. Instead, they began to argue about who was the greatest among them, and Jesus told them, "Whoever receives this child in my name receives me, and whoever receives me receives him who sent me; for he who is least among you all is the one who is great" (Luke 9:48).

It seems that Jesus alone understood what He had to do. It was He alone who knew how much He was going to have to suffer. Luke 9:51 states, "When the days drew near for him to be received up, he set his face to go to Jerusalem." Jesus knew what He had to do in Jerusalem, and He set His face to it. He was resolute. His attitude was, "O.K., let's face it." As He turned toward Jerusalem, there were still those who wanted to follow Him, but they weren't ready or willing to pay the price. The chapter concludes with another amazing statement from the Christ in Luke 9:62, "No one who put his hand to the plow and looks back is fit for the kingdom of God."

What was Jesus doing? He was facing His own cross, His own struggle, and His own fears. We all know what He was setting His face to: His own death. He was going to Jerusalem to be tortured and to be killed. Look at the courage of Jesus! Can we be so resolute? How do we find similar courage to face our trials? When I think about the trials of my own life compared to what Jesus faced, they pale in comparison. Yes, we have had many difficulties with Patrick, but God has been with us through them all. It hasn't always been easy to face the trials, but we have never had to do it alone.

Later in the Gospel of Luke in chapter 21, Jesus has entered the temple and was teaching the people there. Here, Jesus gives us the answer to how we should face our own trials and how we can find courage in the face of difficulty. In Luke 21:36, He says, "But watch at all times, praying that you may have strength to escape all these things that will take place, and to stand before the Son of Man." We must stay awake and be prepared. We must pray for strength and hold our ground. I know that Patrick is going to face many more problems, and I know we will face problems with his brothers and sisters too. For me the strength to face these difficulties must come from prayer and the Sacraments. As I try to prioritize the things I need to accomplish each week, I try to put prayer and frequent daily Mass first. I don't always succeed in getting to Mass or in using my prayer time effectively, but those are always my goals. Ralph Waldo Emerson once said, "Do the thing and you will have the power. But they that do not the thing, had not the power." The thing for me is to try to focus not on the troubles and trials of this life but on the joys of the next. None of us know what challenges the future holds. Thank God. Each of us though needs to look to Jesus for the example of how to deal with those challenges. We need to face it and be faithful.

"I have said this to you, that in me you may have peace.
In the world you have tribulation; but be of good cheer,
I have overcome the world."
John 16:33

Chapter Nine

I See Nothing

November 25, 2001

My Dear Patrick,

The month of November has brought many trips back and forth to Silvercrest. I know it has been hard on you. The plan was to get you used to being at home little by little, adding a day each week until you were home for good. It was also a chance for the school in Loogootee to prepare for everything you need and a time to prepare to care for you at home. During all this Grandma Gibbons came from California to visit us. She was very happy to see you. I don't know if you realize that you have made your last trip. It was just before Thanksgiving. When you came home for Thanksgiving break, you came home to stay. This Thanksgiving, as always, we had much to be thankful for. Daddy and I waited for so long for the time when we would not be taking you back. A few times we came very close only to have the plans change at the last minute. Now you are home. You will not be going back to the school again.

I guess it will take time to help you understand. The trip we took today was very upsetting to you. We went to Louisville to celebrate the feast of Christ the King with some friends. It is the last day of the Church year. Next Sunday begins Advent, a special time set aside to prepare for Christmas. Our trip took us on the highway that goes right past Silvercrest. From the time we headed south you began to cry. No matter how hard we tried to explain to you that we were going to a beautiful Mass and celebration dinner, you continued your usual protest of squealing, crying, and hitting the seat and window.

It was wonderful to have you at Mass. It has become very hard for me to walk with your little brother, Connor, growing inside me. Daddy, as usual, spent most of the Mass walking with you in the back of church or in the cry room. I know the lights, sounds, and smells in the church must be overpowering for you sometimes. You seem to have come up with your own special ways of handling too much coming at you at one time. Daddy often uses deep pressure to help you calm down. I know jumping up and down seems to help too. Today you seemed to tolerate it very well, although I think you enjoyed the dinner even more. They served so many of your favorite foods. I hope you enjoyed it.

On the way home the van was very quiet. Your brothers and sisters slept while you looked out the window into the darkness. It was as though you were looking for a sign, any sign that would tell you where you were headed. Over the years we have taken you many places. Today we took you home. As you sleep soundly in your bed with your brothers you look so peaceful. It is so good to have you home. We pray that you are home to stay, and we ask God to show us how to care for you. Even though you may not be home for good, I will cherish this chance to kiss you good night. God bless you, my little one.

I love you,
Mommy

"Come to me, all who labor and are heavy laden,
and I will give you rest."
Matthew 11:28

As I reached into the oven to pull out the freshly baked muffins, Kate yelled, "They're here!" Our friends had arrived for coffee. No problem. I glanced around the house and couldn't help but think how nice and cozy everything looked on such a cold, blustery fall day. I even had lit candles. But then, just as their car pulled up the driveway, it happened. The sun came out. Rays of sunlight burst through every window in the house and suddenly my nice, clean, cozy house did not seem so clean anymore. The windows looked like someone had been finger-painting on them. Dust bunnies were hopping everywhere, and the Cheerios here and there on the floor looked as big as bagels. I stopped myself just before I panicked and started yelling at the kids, "Quick! Dust the furniture; clean the windows. Scrub the floors, and don't forget the corners."

I was able to relax and smile as I greeted our friends at the door. This was just a small way to practice a lesson God and Patrick had taught me several years before: to keep going cheerfully even when I'm surrounded by more than I think I can handle.

It was a morning after our family campout at—believe it or not—Camp Nothing Much Here. Yes, such a place does exist. When you live in the middle of suburban USA in a new housing development, putting up a tent on some land with trees taller than ten feet becomes roughing it in the wilderness. We had spent two days packing up most everything we owned, and some extra things just in case we might need it and would hate to be caught without. We piled into the van and drove off in the rain to our favorite campsite five miles from our home.

Soon some of our dear friends arrived with their families who were also willing to brave the great outdoors. We set up our tents in the rain. Eventually the rain stopped, and the rest of the campout was filled with rest, relaxation, mud and more mud. Then less than 24 hours later we loaded everything and everyone back into the van for the 5-mile drive home.

It was now time to clean up and put everything away. After hanging several sleeping bags on the clothesline to air out, I stood in my kitchen surrounded by more work than I cared to see. There were piles of laundry, pots, pans, dishes, muddy shoes, and clothes waiting to be washed. Everywhere I looked there were things that needed my attention, including several little children running through the house. The smell of the campfire still clung to everything, along with remnants of sticky marshmallows and chocolate.

Exhausted, I looked out the window to see what Patrick was up to. There in 98 degree whether with nearly 100% humidity was a Winnie the Pooh sleeping bag with two feet hanging out the bottom, swinging on the swing. I left my air-conditioned kitchen and ran back to the swing to try to coax Patrick out of the sleeping bag. As I approached I could hear him giggling with glee as he kicked his feet and swung high into the air. I could not imagine how he could possibly breathe completely enclosed in the sleeping bag, but he seemed so happy flying through the air.

I looked across the yard to a neighbor's house where Mark was 20 feet up on a ladder painting. I knew Mark was struggling to paint in such oppressive heat. I could not imagine how Patrick could continue to breathe, and yet he was so happy. When Mark looked over from the neighbor's house he smiled and said, "That's Patrick." So many things in Patrick's world bother him. He found a way to not have to see or hear anything in the quiet darkness of the sleeping bag, and at the same time to take comfort of the swing. Patrick found a way to make all his irritations seemingly go away.

When I returned to the kitchen, I looked around at all the things that were bothering me, all the piles of dirty things that needed my attention. It would soon be time to fix lunch, and I hadn't even finished the breakfast dishes. Realizing that I could not just escape into a sleeping bag, I began to pray. I felt the Lord was telling me to rest in the comfort of His arms, and there to find peace and joy as though there were nothing that I needed to do—a taste of heaven—then to go and do everything He has set before me with great love and to the best of my ability, knowing that it is by His grace that I can do anything.

When it seems there is just too much to do, when my house seems to have turned upside down and I feel like I'm getting nowhere, I think of a little boy in a Winnie the Pooh sleeping bag, on the swing. I stop. I think of heaven and smile. Then I move on.

"But seek first his kingdom and his righteousness,
and all these things shall be yours as well."
Matthew 6:33

Chapter Ten

Puzzles

December 27, 2001

Dear Patrick,

You've been home for several weeks now, but I'm still writing you letters so you will remember someday everything that has happened. Christmas was wonderful! I didn't know if you would make it through Mass with all of us on Christmas Eve, but you did. I think it helped that I took you to McDonald's for French fries before Mass while Mommy sat with all the other kids. A full tummy usually gives you a better attitude. It works for me too. It was a beautiful evening, and it made me so happy to have us all together. I could see the tears in Mommy's eyes near the end of Mass. It was very special.

It's been great to have you home with us, but it has also been very difficult. We all decided in your last case conference that you needed an extended school day to keep working on improving your behavior and other skills. We have had such a hard time trying to get people to come to our home after school to work with you though. We don't have the room for someone to work with you one on one undisturbed, and you get so upset in the evenings. We've been through several people already. They are good people; it's just that you are so hard to work with. We were supposed to have respite care for you over the Christmas break also, but the agency hasn't been able to find anyone to staff it. It's not that we want you away from us. It's just that it is so much better for you to be able to go off with someone to the pool or park where you can get rid of some of your energy.

The other kids love having you home, but they've grown scared of you. I know you don't want to hear that, and I know you don't want to hurt them. I see the frustration and pain in your eyes when you hit one of the kids or me. You try to stop yourself, but you just can't. I've been really frightened that you are really going to hurt one of the little ones or Mommy. Mommy is due any day now with baby Connor, so she has had to stay away from you for the most part. We just can't take the chance that you will hurt her. I wish we could find some way to stop all your aggression, Patrick. If we could just find some way to keep you from getting upset, things could run so much more smoothly.

I was really sad a couple weeks ago when you hurt Cary. He's an old friend of mine from high school and college who agreed to work with you in the evenings. He worked so well with you too before you injured him. I'm sure you didn't mean to hurt him. It was so much easier when you were small, Patrick. I didn't worry about you hurting others because you were always so gentle. I know you don't have any other way to communicate your feelings, but it is getting frightening.

Some day you will be perfected, Patrick. We may never see it in this life, but because of Christmas Day, because Jesus came into the world, we have hope that you will one day be perfect in heaven. I know you will be there, Patrick. As I pray for you tonight, I pray that Daddy will be able to join you there too. It is a thought and hope that sustains me as I pray for you this night. God bless you, buddy.

I love you,
Daddy

"Let us then with confidence draw near to the throne of grace, that we may receive mercy and find grace in time of need."

Hebrews 4:16

Life does get crazy now and then in our household. There are times when things aren't perfectly clean or when everyone is so busy it's hard to keep track of our schedules. Often Beth or I have meetings in the evening at church or in the community, and like most everyone else raising a family, it is difficult to remain calm and focused. One such day of craziness was the September day when our third daughter and seventh child, Bridget, was born. I came home from football practice knowing that Beth may need to go to the hospital at any time. Because of her many complications, the doctors often induce labor early.

Any teacher will tell you that during the course of the school day we have dozens of tasks to accomplish. We've got papers to grade, lessons to plan, parents to phone, messages to answer, e-mails to write, committee meetings to attend, and even students to teach. You get the picture. I was trying to get things ready for a substitute teacher the next day because we were pretty sure that Bridget was coming soon. Planning for a substitute is quite often more work than actually showing up and teaching for the day. It's hard to convey what another needs to accomplish to make the day worthwhile. In any case, I had worked very hard that day to see that everything was done. If this was the day, all I would have to do is come home, throw a few things in the overnight bag, take the rest of the kids down the street to stay with our friends, the Bullocks, until my parents could get to our house, and take a leisurely fall drive to St. Vincent's Hospital. Or so I thought. As usual, Patrick had a different plan.

Earlier that afternoon Beth had gone to see her doctor for a routine checkup. While she was there, the doctor decided to schedule her for an amniocentesis to see if Bridget's lungs were developed enough for an induction. As I got home, Beth called from the hospital to say that the results were good, and the doctor wanted to keep her at the hospital and induce labor. I told her that Patrick had been pulling on his stomach and appeared to be in pain. That much wasn't new. Patrick often had stomach discomfort, and we had treated him with medication and diet over the years in efforts to help him.

This was somehow different though. He was moaning and sobbing. Most children, of course, can tell you if their stomach is truly upset or if their side is hurting. Patrick cannot, and so it is up to us to do the detective work. Beth had talked to the doctor earlier in the afternoon about Patrick's pain. Patrick was being slowly weaned from a medication that can cause flu-like symptoms if it is done too quickly. When Patrick came home from school that day, the pain seemed much worse. I phoned his doctor, and he suggested that I take Patrick to the emergency room to have him checked out for a possible appendicitis attack. He was certain he had weaned Patrick from his medication appropriately.

Patrick hated having blood drawn as most children would. He has gotten quite used to it now, but at that time, it was a major struggle. I had to hold him down in the emergency room while they drew the vials of blood and then again when he was taken to radiology for x-rays. While waiting on results I phoned my parents who lived two and a half hours away to see if they could come to stay with the kids as it looked like Beth was going to have Bridget soon. I struggled to explain to them that I was at one hospital with Patrick while Beth was at another quite possibly in labor. Patrick continued to moan and squeal as I walked up and down the halls of the hospital with him, but the tests proved inconclusive. They dismissed us, and I took Patrick home. By the time my parents arrived at our house Patrick had calmed down enough for me to leave him and the rest of the kids and head off to be with Beth who was now in full labor. I have no idea what was going on with him, but by the time I joined Beth at the hospital it was about eleven o'clock, and I was exhausted. Fortunately, I didn't miss Bridget's birth. She wasn't born until the next morning, and Patrick seemed fine.

One of my frustrations with Patrick has always been trying to figure out all the unknowns. I want to know how he is feeling and what he is thinking. I want to know if he is happy or feeling down, and I just don't know. Patrick has never been able to tell me if he is happy or sad. Sometimes I can tell when he needs something, but not always. Try though we may, there are so many unknowns.

We have used medication to try to help Patrick with those things that we cannot see. Patrick has undergone just about every test imaginable to try to determine what's going on inside his body. He has had EKGs and EEGs, x-rays of all sorts, blood tests, allergy tests, CAT scans, and even a brain spectroscopy. No matter the tests, whatever is going on inside his body remains essentially a mystery to us. We've tried so many different kinds of medication and so many therapies. Some have shown moderate success; others have done little or nothing. We continue to try, however, because we want to do all we can to cooperate with God's plan for him.

So often my cooperation with God comes in the form of grace through the Sacraments, particularly Penance and Reconciliation. Few have eyes to see any exterior signs of my sin, but God sees it, and if I am attentive, I will see it too. As we have used medication to try to help Patrick, God uses His grace to rid me of my sin and to heal me. Experience shows me that many of my problems stem from sins I haven't confessed. It is vital to my own well being that I do so. In fact, I must. Going to Confession with our children has become a priority for our family. The kids even seem to look forward to our Saturday journeys. I try to recognize the channels of grace that God has provided, and Beth likes me a whole lot better when I've just come home from the Sacrament. The grace is free. I just have to get in line.

"Whoever then relaxes one of the least of these commandments and teaches men so, shall be called least in the kingdom of heaven; but he who does them and teaches them shall be called great in the kingdom of heaven."

Matthew 5:19

CHAPTER ELEVEN

The Bath

February 3, 2002

My Dear Patrick,

Today was a very special day for our family. Your brother Connor John was baptized. It is great to have Sean home for a few days. Tomorrow he will fly back to Center Harbor. I have enjoyed seeing the two of you together again. He is Connor's godfather, and Laura is his godmother. We gave your baby brother the name Connor John after the late John Cardinal O'Connor of New York. He believed all children are precious gifts from God, and he had great compassion for those with special needs. His life was a beautiful example of hard work and dedication out of love for Christ.

By the time Connor was born I had been unable to walk for about six weeks. I have many physical problems that make it very hard the last few months of pregnancy, but I would not trade it for the world. The time passes so quickly, and before I know it I have another little miracle in my arms. I can still remember the last few weeks before I gave birth to you. I spent them hand sewing little stuffed teddy bears for your wall. I know you must see them every day. I don't think I ever told you where they came from. They always remind me of the beautiful gift you are.

Connor came into the world on January 11th. Do you remember that day? Grandma and Aunt Mary Lou came over to take care of you and your brothers and sisters while Daddy took me to the hospital. Becky spent part of the evening with you too. She has done so much to try to help you, and I think the two of you have a lot of fun together, running through the fields and playing on the swing. I think she will be spending some time with you again tomorrow.

We have been watching you much more closely now since you had the grand mal seizure. A few weeks ago Daddy took you to St. Vincent Hospital in Indianapolis to have a test done called a video EEG. Do you remember how Daddy explained that it checks to see if you need medication to prevent more seizures? You didn't seem to care that they hooked your head up to many wires and taped them all on. I think the 24-hour test was harder on Daddy than it was on you. You seemed to like lying in bed, enjoying the two suitcases full of toys and videos I sent along. We will have to wait and talk to the doctor about the results when we see him in a few weeks.

This has been a very special weekend for me. Not only because of Connor's baptism, but because all ten of my children are home. It is so wonderful to have our family together again. Yesterday we had a family picture taken so we can remember this time when everyone was home. It may not come again, and so for the gift of today, having you here to hold, I am very grateful. God bless you, my little one.

I love you,
Mommy

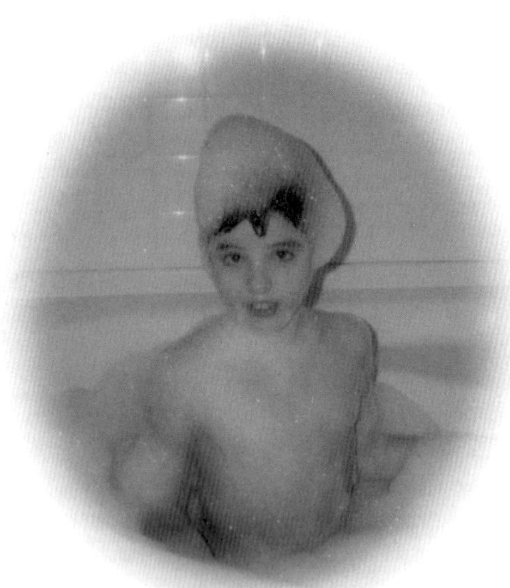

"Do not be conformed to this world, but be transformed by the renewal of your mind, that you may prove what is the will of God, what is good and acceptable and perfect."

Romans 12:2

Patrick jumped around the bathroom while I began to fill the tub with warm water for his bath. Every once in a while he would pause and look up above the tub. I knew there was no way he would get into the tub until I covered with a towel one of the few things in this world that we knew terrified him: the showerhead. Patrick did not like showers and would soak in the tub for hours as long as he could not see what was lurking above him. I covered the showerhead with a towel, and Patrick jumped right in. The bath was one of his favorite places to be day or night. It made him feel good.

Soon it would be time to get Patrick out of the tub to begin his usual before bed struggle. First comes his diaper secured with black electrical tape, then his pajama sleeper on backwards with a safety pin at the top of the zipper. This was the best we could come up with to keep him warm on cold winter nights. Patrick would not keep covers on and in seconds could remove any piece of clothing, no matter how many snaps, buttons, or zippers. Wearing clothing was torture to Patrick. Like the saints of old who would wear hair shirts under their clothes to deny themselves comfort, clothing caused Patrick constant discomfort or pain.

We had just begun a new treatment for Patrick called brush therapy. It is a way to desensitize his skin to the sense of touch. During different times throughout his day we would brush his skin, mostly his arms and legs, with a surgical brush. As a result, Patrick slowly began to tolerate the feeling of fabric on his skin. Even now he continues to receive brush therapy and does not seem to have any trouble wearing his clothes.

As I brush Patrick's skin I am often reminded of an old proverb of cooking a frog. If you put a frog in a pan of cold water, he will jump out. If you put him in a pan of boiling water, he will jump out. To cook a frog you must put him in a pan of warm water. He will like the warm water and want to stay. Slowly while the frog is enjoying the warm water you turn up the temperature. The warmth of the water paralyzes the frog's muscles, and he cannot move. When the frog realizes that the warm bath he has been enjoying is no longer a pleasant experience, he is stuck. He cannot jump out of the same boiling water that earlier he would have hopped right out of. He becomes desensitized to the boiling water until it's too late.

I wonder how many things I've become desensitized to. The main one that comes to mind is television. I know that my grandfather would not have stood for one second of what in many cases is considered good family entertainment today. He was a noble man of principle, and the television would have ended up in the trash. The family shows can be better than many other programs, but are they actually good? Or am I being desensitized to go one step further and think, "It's not that bad." It's like a new watch that drove me crazy the first few days I wore it. Now I have become so accustomed to it that I have to look to see if I'm wearing it.

So many things in this world seem to be brushing against my conscience, like the surgical brush against Patrick's skin. One thing after another bears the message, "It's not so bad once you get used to it." Patrick's skin needs to be desensitized; my conscience does not. The frog in the water needs to look under the pot to see the source of his comfortable warm water is a raging hot fire that will cause him extreme pain and eventually death. Watching Patrick soak in the warm tub, reminds me that like the frog, I too must wake up and look for the source of my comfort, and be sure it is only one fire, the burning fire of Christ's love.

"Not every one who says to me, 'Lord, Lord,' shall enter the kingdom of heaven, but he who does the will of my Father who is in heaven."

Matthew 7:21

Chapter Twelve

Working Day and Night

March 28, 2002

Dear Patrick,

Spring Break is upon us again. The weather is warming up a little, but we are almost too busy to enjoy it. March has been an eventful month to say the least.

We met with a new special needs agency and advocate, Becky, to see what they could do to help us get the services you need. Becky has been wonderful. She understands your situation really well and knows the people to contact for help. The past few months have been so hard on all of us. It's been great to have you home, but the little ones keep getting hurt, and you get so frustrated. The clock has been ticking, and you're just not getting any better. School has been going well with Mrs. Frye, but the situation at home keeps getting harder and harder.

As each case conference passed, we kept getting more and more dejected. We would check on your spot on the waiver waiting list, and it was moving up instead of down. Then God sent Mommy and me to Evansville for a very important meeting, and a miracle has happened. We are going to be able to get a waiver for you.

That Friday night was dreary and cold, and we couldn't find where the meeting was being held. When we finally got there, it had already begun, so we moved up to the front where there were a couple seats. When the presentation was over, we listened to parents ask questions that sounded all too familiar. Nearly everyone had a sad story to tell about how they couldn't get the necessary services for their sons or daughters. We stayed late to ask the presenter a few questions, and she surprised us with her answers. It seems she had heard of you, Patrick. Several people had contacted her office about the difficulties you were having. I'm sure that many more have been praying for you. Whatever the case, God has put us in touch with the people who will be able to help you. We are so thankful to God because this means that we will now be able to get you so much more help to provide for your needs. And you won't have to go to Kansas to get it!

I will be taking you to the hospital tomorrow for an EKG. I know you don't like going to the doctor or hospital because you never know what to expect. Dr. Aull wants to try some new medication, and we need to find out some things about your heart. It won't be too bad. The last time we went to the hospital you had to stay overnight, and I know you didn't like that. This time won't take long. It sounds like things are really coming together, and we'll just keep praying that everything works according to God's plan. I love you.

Love,
Dad

"And whatever you do, in word or deed, do everything in the name of the Lord Jesus, giving thanks to God the Father through Him."

Colossians 3:17

I walked quietly into Patrick's classroom as I do most every day. I like to check on him during the day when I can find the time. Patrick stood next to a table sorting out and counting little beads. Next, he placed the multi-colored beads into opened plastic eggs in groups of ones, twos, threes, and fours. He was working on counting and sorting by color much as he has done each school day for the past five years. To most it would seem that Patrick's skill level hasn't improved much over time, but very slowly he is making progress. Usually he is very patient as he goes through this routine, one that he has repeated hundreds of times. It is part of his normal work schedule, and it's a painstaking task. He doesn't always get it right. Some days he is more successful than others just like me in my daily work, just like all of us in daily tasks.

The life and work of St. José Maria Escriva has always appealed to me. The founder of Opus Dei, St. Escriva taught that work could be a means of our sanctification. He taught that our daily tasks were a means to individual holiness. Our work makes up so much of our daily activities; it makes perfect sense to try to become more holy through our labor. In addition, Pope John Paul II noted in a homily on May 8, 1988 that, "Work...is not something that people do for the sole purpose of earning a living; it is a human dimension that can and must be sanctified, in order to bring people to the total fulfillment of their vocation as creatures made in the image and likeness of God."

I think about this often as I make my way through the daily rigors of living. If I don't see my work as somehow edifying, it makes it much more difficult to accomplish. Much of what we do on a regular basis is mundane. I don't know many people who are constantly energized and enthused by their work and home routines. In fact, it is far more common to hear complaints from co-workers and friends. Why do people often seem so unhappy? I suspect it is because we've lost the sense of purpose for what we do. I would imagine that about everyone has seen the bracelets, T-shirts, and posters emblazoned with WWJD. We've been asked to consider what Jesus would do in any given situation to help direct and guide our decisions.

Perhaps an equally good question is, "What did Jesus do?" Specifically, what did He do during those years we know so little of His life?

After Jesus was found in the temple at age 12, we know very little about Him until his public ministry. Luke 2:52 states, "Jesus grew both in height and wisdom, and He was loved by God and all who knew Him." That is very little information. We are told that Mary stored all these things in her heart, but little is recorded of what she stored. So we are left to imagine what these hidden years of Jesus were like. I think it is most likely that Jesus was engaged in manual labor in St. Joseph's workshop. He went to synagogue and prayed. No doubt he talked with people and was a good neighbor. He probably worked with other apprentices and tried to find ways to do his job better. He did not marry which would have been unusual for His time.

We can assume that St. Joseph died during those years because no mention is made of Joseph during the public ministry of Jesus. Jesus would have likely slowly taken the place of his foster-father while Joseph's health failed. No doubt He grieved when Joseph died and continued to take care of His mother, Mary. He would have been a just worker, a friend to children and strangers, and a good, patient man. In other words, He wasn't too dissimilar from many of His neighbors and townspeople. Hopefully, He wasn't too dissimilar from us either. What Jesus did during these years was every bit as much a part of God's plan for His life as was His public ministry. It was during these years that He truly grew in height and wisdom like all of us. I suspect that most of us can relate to this Jesus who worked and helped take care of His family. The little, everyday tasks helped prepare Him for His ministry. He was very much like us in all ways except sin.

When I struggle with my daily problems: tiresome work, unpaid bills, interrupted sleep, or car problems, it helps me to reflect on "what Jesus did." If I really do what Jesus did, all of these problems would be occasions to help me grow in wisdom and, more importantly, holiness. It also helps me to reflect on Patrick's life. I can't imagine a more repetitive life than his. Patrick is still working on the same rudimentary tasks he worked on as a four and five year old. He is still counting objects and matching colors. He is still struggling to mimic words from a speech therapist and put puzzle pieces in their places. He is still working to master simple tasks like tying his shoes, brushing his teeth, and typing a sentence. These are all tasks that have varied little over the past ten years, and yet he rarely complains or whines. I wonder how much patience I would have if my life were so seemingly dull. Yes, Patrick has his times of frustration and misbehavior, but who wouldn't? If he understands as much as I think he does, I can only imagine that it gets very tedious and tiresome to repeat the same tasks over and over again.

As I contemplate the life of Jesus during those hidden years from 12 to 30, I know that those years of growth were of great importance. Those years must have had as much value as his three years of preaching. Our daily lives have great importance too. Day by day we must grow in holiness. Day by day we must accomplish the tasks that God places before us even if, like Patrick, they seem routine and boring. The depth of meaning in our daily lives is difficult to see because it is so repetitive. Perhaps some day we will understand the importance of our work and family lives as we strive to become more holy and bring our loved ones to a deeper relationship with Christ. We must learn to put meaning into our daily lives to be truly happy. We must try to do what Jesus did. WDJD?

"Rejoice in that day, and leap for joy, for behold,
your reward is great in heaven."
Luke 6:23

Chapter Thirteen

Danger Zone

May 1, 2002

My Dear Patrick,

Today has been a very emotional day for me. It has been a day mixed with both happiness and sadness. Today we moved you into your own special little house. I pray you will be happy there. It has been very hard to move your things out. I hoped this day would never come, and yet I knew it had to. It is not safe for you to live at home now, so we've found you a place where you can hopefully get the help that you need. When the state department of education rejected your application for the school in Kansas, we could not imagine that God had something better in mind, but as always He did.

It will be much better than having you so far away from us. We can come and see you anytime we want. We will be able to go swimming with you at the YMCA, and have pizza with you. Pizza always tastes better when you are with us. Best of all, your classroom at school will still be down the hall from Daddy, so he can see you everyday.

The search for a house for you has been very hard. Many evenings Daddy and I took you for a ride through the streets of Washington looking for a house. It was very discouraging. There were very few houses to look at, and we could not find any that weren't near busy streets or railroad tracks. The fact that you like to lie in the street and touch cars definitely limits our choices.

After several meetings with people who are trying to help you, like Monica, Gayle, and Abby, we finally have found a place. It is only temporary though. A few weeks ago we met with a man named Denny. He showed us a wooded lot tucked away on a dead end street. He said that he would build a small house there for you. It will be quiet and safe. There are no cars racing past. We don't know when the house will be built, but it sounds very exciting. For now the one you are moving into will have to do. I think you will like it. Becky will be there a lot of the time to help you and take care of you. So will Jenny and Joe. Daddy will be with you tonight and will take you to school in the morning.

I pray your first night away from home is a peaceful one. You seem so far away, and yet since Daddy is with you, I know you are not afraid. I miss you already, my little one.

I love you,
Mommy

"I do not understand my own actions. For I do not do what I want, but I do the very thing I hate."

Romans 7:15

I was standing in the church parking lot after a weekday morning Mass and thought I had a tight hold on Patrick's hand. It wasn't nearly tight enough. At four, Patrick was incredibly strong and fast. He pulled away from me and started running straight toward an oncoming car. I'm sure that to the driver he looked like a child who was old enough to know not to step out in front of a car. What the driver didn't know was that Patrick planned to do just that: step in front of his car. I knew what Patrick was up to, and I also knew that I could not get to him fast enough. I gasped as Patrick darted in front of the car; there was barely time for a quick prayer. As always, his angels must have been protecting him, because the car was able to come to a screeching halt just as Patrick reached out to touch the shiny bumper.

I ran toward Patrick, and I could hear the driver yelling, "Get away from my car." Over and over he yelled, and Patrick just stood there giggling and running his hand over the bumper. He seemed totally oblivious to all the commotion around him. It had been only seconds since Patrick had run toward the car, and yet as I grabbed him and lifted him up into my arms, it seemed like hours. As the car took off, I stood there holding Patrick tightly. I was too frightened to cry, as the horror of what could have happened raced through my mind, along with the realization that the danger would always be there. It was real, even if Patrick couldn't see it.

This was not the first time, and I knew it would not be the last. Patrick has a strong attraction for cars and streets without any understanding of the danger tied to them. Another time, when Patrick was three, he got away from me at the ballpark. I was standing with some of my friends watching our children, while our husbands played softball in our parish league. The children were playing on swings and slides in an area next to the field. It was the bottom of the last inning when I suddenly realized that Patrick was missing. Usually this would mean that Patrick was climbing the slide, or into some one's diaper bag looking for food. Not this time. We searched everywhere for him. It seemed as if he had vanished into thin air. Just as the game ended, and the dads started to help with the search, I spotted his shoe sticking out from behind the tire of a car. When I looked under the car, there was Patrick sound asleep with a look of peace and comfort on his face. It was a hot day, and I'm sure it was the coolest place he could find to take a nap. I shuddered to think what could have happened if the driver of the car tried to drive off before we had found Patrick.

These frightening maneuvers of Patrick's that make my heart skip a beat with fear don't seem to bother Patrick in the least. Many times after a particularly dangerous moment, I hold Patrick in my arms, thanking God, and thinking "What if?" During these moments God has helped me to compare the way Patrick reacts in the face of danger with the way that I react in the face of sin. I don't like my sins, and I'm sorry for them, but what I don't understand, and what really bothers me, is why I don't gasp in horror. I wonder, is the temptation to sin too great like Patrick's temptation to touch a shiny bumper, or is it that I am totally oblivious to the terrible destruction and possibly even death that sin causes? There is a very good chance that it is a combination of both.

I used to think that I would be much more conscious of the horror and ugliness of sin if I wore it on my face for all to see. What I've come to understand is that it would be pointless because I would be motivated to avoid sin, not by love for Christ, but by vanity and pride. I would not want others to see the ugly side of me. The effects of original Sin blur my vision and prevent me from seeing the true horrors of sin. And yet, when I look through the lenses of faith, a faith nurtured by prayer and the Sacraments, I can see clearly that the face of a holy, grace-filled person is beautiful and filled with peace, as compared to the face of someone burdened by the heavy weight of sin.

The more clearly I see sin for what it truly is, the less attractive it becomes. I have also learned that I cannot make others see sin for what it really is. I can only teach them the truth and pray for them. God has shown me this through Patrick. If Patrick cannot see the danger, we can only surround him with our love and protection and pray for his safety. This has become harder and harder the older and stronger he has gotten.

Car rides became much more dangerous when Patrick outgrew his car seat. We tried every kind we could find, and he always found a way out. One time when he was about seven, he gave us quite a scare. We were driving on the highway at night with all the children in the van, when we came to a stop at a traffic light. Patrick dove for the door, opened it, and my arm grabbed him just as he started to jump. We could only wonder what it was he was after.

Just a few weeks before he had run from me in the front yard to the street in front of our house and dropped down on the center white line. It was dark, and I could see the lights of a truck coming down the street. I yelled for Patrick, but he just lay there motionless staring at the white line. Patrick's angels were once again there to protect him. The driver of the truck was our neighbor Caeser, and Mark was riding with him. They were going very slowly and knew to watch for Patrick. The thought of being hit by a truck must have never crossed his mind, because he didn't move until they lifted him out of the road. In his own little world, the white line was all he could see, and it brought him much pleasure.

Just as I need to strive for a clearer vision of sin, I have often thought it would be wonderful if only I could find glasses that would help Patrick see more clearly the danger that surrounds him. Maybe then he would be safe. Maybe then he would see the danger of cars and streets. Until then the Lord keeps telling me to learn from Patrick. Patrick is teaching me in his own special way. He is teaching me to look for the dangers where before I saw only pride, pleasures, and self-gratification.

My daughter Laura marvels at her improved vision after a slight change in her contact prescription. Like her, my vision improves little by little, nurtured by prayer and the Sacraments, helping me to see more clearly with eyes of faith. Some day I pray I will fully see my sins for what they are and recoil from the horror of sin. Until then I can be sure that, just as I want to wrap my arms around Patrick to keep him safe, my Heavenly Father has his loving arms of mercy around me, protecting me from what I cannot yet see. Keeping me safe.

"...that the God of our Lord Jesus Christ, the Father of glory, may give you a spirit of wisdom and of revelation in the knowledge of him, having the eyes of your hearts enlightened, that you may know what is the hope to which He has called you, what are the riches of His glorious inheritance in the saints."

Ephesians 1:17-18

CHAPTER FOURTEEN

Discernment

June 16, 2002

Dear Patrick,

It has been great to be able to stay with you at your new house. I can't imagine a better set up for you right now. You have really enjoyed the aboveground pool in the backyard. Watching you swim is incredible! I don't think I've ever seen you so happy as when you are in water. As I think back to when you taught yourself to swim, I am still so amazed. We tried for so long to get you to cooperate with the instructors, but you had your own ideas. No one would call your form classic, but as I watch your strong body knife through the water I can't help but smile.

We have the results from your allergy tests. As we suspected, you have some major allergies. We had thought for so long that you had some environmental issues, but we could never really pinpoint things. Your new doctor is really good. She tells us that you are allergic to wheat, dust mites, corn, peanuts, and soybeans. We have to put you on a restricted diet. Do you know how many foods have corn, soybeans, and wheat? It's just about everything. I know you aren't going to be too happy about this because you love bread so much. Just about all your favorite snacks have corn or corn syrup. It will be a challenge to keep you on this diet, but without your brothers and sisters around eating foods that you can't have, it should be easier.

Mommy's book about you has been out about three weeks now. So many people have been inspired by your story. I still marvel at how God is working through your life. Even though you can't tell your story of what a blessing you are to us and to the world, people are still learning from you. I think that everyone can relate to the problems you have. They may not be autistic and non-verbal, but they do have other difficulties. Everyone faces some sort of trial, some kind of suffering. It may be cancer or disease, the loss of a loved one or financial problems, but we all suffer. I hope and pray that people may learn to accept their crosses through your story and remember that God loves and cares for them.

A couple weeks ago we went to a conference, and my back was hurting so much. The only way I could get it to stop hurting was to lie flat, but there was no place to do that. I don't know what's wrong, but I can hardly stand or sit. Dr. Nonte has been trying to help me feel better, but it doesn't seem to be helping. He has helped me a lot in the past, so this must be something different. If I have learned anything from seeing your suffering, it is that I need to accept my suffering as small as it is. You've been through so much more than a bad back. I think about your inability to talk, your seizures, your dietary restrictions, your frustrations, and I realize that I have nothing to complain about. You have taught me patience and unconditional love. Thank you, Patrick.

I love you,
Dad

"And because you hearken to these ordinances, and keep and do them, the Lord your God will keep with you the covenant and the steadfast love which He swore to your fathers to keep; He will love you, bless you, and multiply you; he will also bless the fruit of your body and the fruit of your ground..."

Deuteronomy 6:12-13

"Six of one. Half a dozen of another." I don't know how many times my dad or someone else has told me that when I have had to make a choice between two equally good opportunities. It's so difficult as parents to know what is best for our children. I find myself praying for discernment on many occasions. Should we allow Sean to go to an apostolic school in New Hampshire, or should he stay with us? Should Beth and I go against the norms and home school our children or send them to a really good school in our hometown? Should I accept the offer of a new job or stay with the one I have? We all face similar choices throughout our lives. How do we know what is best?

With Patrick it has been especially difficult. Often we have received contradictory suggestions or ideas for treatment. Doctors who work with children on the autism spectrum have many theories about the best methods of treatment. Since I'm not a health professional or special education teacher, I usually have no idea what course to take. Many options sound reasonable and credible. We have had doctors tell us that Patrick needs to be on a special diet to help control his behavior. Others saw no correlation between diet and behavior and prescribed medication instead. One doctor was convinced that Patrick had severe stomach problems and should be treated with an anti-fungal medication. Another believed that we needed somehow to teach him to hear properly and recommended auditory training. Some educational specialists have advised us to use Applied Behavioral Analysis (ABA), but none can agree on how it should be done. Teachers, doctors, and therapists all seem to favor one treatment or another depending upon what conference they've recently attended or under whom they have studied. How do we know what to do? It seems I always come back to this crucial question.

A generation ago many believed that frigid mothers caused autism. They called it "Refrigerator Mothers." The theory was that somehow children who were neglected or rejected by their mothers turned inward and developed communication and social disorders. I cannot imagine how difficult this was for mothers so accused. More recently it has been popular to look at vaccinations, specifically the Measles, Mumps, Rubella, as a possible cause for autistic behavior. Some parents, therefore, are hesitant to have their children immunized against these diseases, and they can find doctors on both sides of the issue. It's enough to drive parents crazy.

All parents want what is best for their children. In my experience as a classroom teacher for nearly two decades I've never met a parent who purposely chose a medical treatment or educational plan they believed was going to harm their child. Certainly, there are sick individuals who do inflict unnecessary punishment or pain upon their children through abuse or neglect, but that is rare. Millions, if not billions, of dollars are spent yearly trying to persuade parents to do the right things for their children. We're bombarded with advertisements to convince us to buy everything from the proper juice or sports drink to the best educational toys and games. We're coerced into believing that we should send our children to the finest summer camps and the best schools. Commercial jingles replay in our heads, and newspaper and magazine ads accost us with their lavish promises. We probably all succumb to some of that media blitz in one way or another. I know I have taken it to heart because I "deserve a break today" and need to "have it my way."

No doubt we all know someone who has agonized over a decision regarding his or her children. Sometimes parents come to Beth or me for advice, and we, of course, try to help them discern what path to choose. Too often, however, someone will call us distraught over the course of action they have already chosen. They'll lament that it seemed like a good idea at the time but just isn't working the way they had hoped. Believe me.

We've been there too. At that point Beth often says, "We do the best we can for our children at that time with what we know all the while trusting that God will take care of them." I suspect that all of our parents did things differently from us. Many parents were told to lay their babies on their stomachs; research has shown that has been a contributor to Sudden Infant Death Syndrome. Most pediatricians used to recommend giving small children a baby aspirin for a fever; that's no longer believed to be true. In fact, it may even be deadly. Our parents put us in hard shoes convinced that was what we needed to learn how to walk. Now we believe that they shouldn't wear shoes at all. One generation turned to Dr. Spock. Ours has turned to Dr. Laura and Dr. Phil.

There are so many avenues that we have traveled with Patrick that we probably would not travel again if given a second chance. In all cases we have prayed for guidance, and we have tried to make decisions based upon what we felt God was asking of us. We have prayed that God lead us to the right doctors, the right schools, and the right therapists. As much as we know about autism, we are really just scratching the surface. And the same can be said for many other diseases or conditions. In fact, as much as we think we know about the world and each other, we still know so little.

So many of us believe that we know it all. We have the Internet for instant communication, satellite television for immediate knowledge of world events, and beepers in case we are away from either. We think we have all the answers, but in many ways the simple farmer and tradesmen of centuries ago knew so much more. They knew what it meant to be dependent upon God. Job, for example, knew the source of all his blessings. After Job had lost children and possessions he said, "Naked I came from my mother's womb, and naked shall I return; the Lord gave, and the Lord has taken away; blessed be the name of the Lord" (Job 1:21). Obviously, Job was right.

Most of my ancestors probably could not have explained complicated theological issues. Nor did they know much of worldly pursuits. What they did know was hard work, love of family, and faith in God. Because of them, I am who I am. Their sacrifices, and the sacrifices of others, made possible the life I lead today. I reflect often about how the Faith was handed down to me. I have no idea who the first Christian in my family was, but I suspect it was as long as 1500 years ago in Ireland. Many times my ancestors have sacrificed to hand on the faith to the succeeding generation. And each generation has continued to pass that torch of faith until it was passed from my parents to me. It is incumbent upon me to see that it is passed on to my own children, to see that I don't drop the torch.

Quite simply, the more I know, the more I know that I don't know much. God does know, though. He has a plan for each of our lives and the lives of all of our children and loved ones. He knows and loves us deeply. He wants us to seek Him always, and for that reason I must be deeply rooted in prayer. Prayer is the primary way that I will ever be able to discern any of the decisions I have to make about Patrick or any of our children. Certainly, I consult the advice of other professionals, seek the guidance of family and friends, and read what others have written, but prayer is where these many voices come together. I just pray that my family and I keep our focus on heaven and not on things of this world. Now what was that again? "Feed a cold and starve a fever? Or starve a cold and feed a fever?"

"The kingdom of heaven is like treasure hidden in a field, which a man found and covered up; then in his joy he goes and sells all that he has and buys that field."

Matthew 13:44

Chapter Fifteen

The Carousel

June 28, 2002

My Dear Patrick,

My goodness what a wonderful day today has been! It was great to be together as a family for a day of fun at Holiday World. A few years ago when we went you could not go with us. Someone gave our family tickets to the amusement park as a gift so we could take you and the whole family. We even had a ticket so that Aaron could come along to help you. It is so hard for Daddy to take care of you with his bad back. Hopefully the doctor will be able to fix it soon. Dr. Hoffman is doing all he can to help Daddy.

I can remember riding next to you on a ride called the Scrambler. At first you giggled with anticipation, but as the ride moved faster I could feel your body next to mine just relaxing and enjoying it. Your eyes were closed, and you were smiling, lost in the moment. The peace and joy that overcame you was something I seldom see. At that moment, I wanted to keep you there forever. It reminded me so much of when you were a baby. You always seemed so content. We didn't get to stay on the ride forever, but they did let you stay one more turn.

Another ride was a great big swing called the Banshee. It sure is bigger than your tree swing. Sean was home from school on a short break and took you on it, and like before they let you stay on for two turns. The park gave you a VIP pass so you didn't have to wait in lines. I know you are a very important person, but it isn't often that the world recognizes it. Sean even took you on one of their big roller coasters, but I don't think you enjoyed that ride as much as the others.

My favorite place to take you was the water park. It was a little too crowded for you, but I think you enjoyed it anyway. Even with all the different water rides to choose from I think you had the most fun just playing in the water in one of the many pools. No matter where you are, when you find your way to water it makes you happy. You are quite the little fish. It has been a beautiful day, one that I'm sure to remember.

Now that Sean is home for summer break, we will be coming to your house to visit and swim with you as often as we can. Patrick, you are his special little brother, and he misses you so much. It was wonderful that the two of you could spend the day together. Daddy will be with you again tonight, and I will see you soon. God bless you, my little one.

I love you,
Mommy

"As obedient children do not be conformed to the passions of your former ignorance, but as He who called you is holy, be holy yourselves in all of your conduct."

1 Peter 1:14-15

I jumped out of the car and ran into one of our local small town restaurants where my husband Mark was having a planning meeting for his twenty-year high school class reunion. As I approached their table, his friends looked rather startled, but Mark did not. He had learned to expect the unexpected. Wasting no time, I quickly blurted out, "The plans have changed. In a half hour you need to be over at the Little League field for Michael's game. First, go home and pick up Sean and Brendan. After Michael's game run over and see how Megan's game is going at the softball field. When Megan's game is over, you and Megan need to go back to the other field to watch the end of Brendan's game. I've got the baby with me, and I'm dropping Megan off at the softball field on the way to my meeting. Laura has the other kids at home." Mark, as usual, was amazing. He smiled and gave me a simple o.k. That simple o.k. really means, "I've heard everything you have said, and I understand the plan. Enjoy your meeting." I was off and running.

I didn't want to change the plans we had made for the evening. It just happened. How was I to know that just as I was leaving for my meeting, Megan's softball coach would call and say that they are making up a rained-out game in forty-five minutes, that they are short on players, and that they really need Megan? The hard part was that Megan and Brendan had been sharing cleats because Megan's were missing shoestrings. As we ran out the door I had Megan grab a pair of tennis shoes, hoping the strings would work in her cleats. The strings worked great, and somehow Mark got everyone where they needed to be when they needed to be there. He even told me later that it was fun!

So goes another evening in the Matthews home. It seems day after day that we run around to different activities and meetings. It's enough to make my head spin. At times when I've taken my crazy day to the Lord in prayer, asking Him to help me get it all done, I close my eyes and remember Patrick on a carousel. Then I hear the Lord gently reminding me, "You don't have to stay on, Beth. The painted ponies are beautiful and fun to ride. They may even go up and down, but if they are not bringing you closer to Me, then it's time to get off."

Patrick loves carousels. His favorite is in the Children's Museum of Indianapolis. Going round and round in circles actually has a calming effect on him. Once, when he was about four, we went to a carnival. There were rides everywhere, every ride you could imagine. Yet Patrick only wanted to ride the carousel. Not only does it go up and down and around, but also it has horses. Like many autistic children, Patrick loves horses. A kind man who was working at the carousel could see how much Patrick liked it and said he could ride as long as he liked. He even offered to ride with him. I tried many times to get Patrick to look at other rides, but he would not budge from his horse. He was happy just where he was and rode for well over an hour before he decided it was time to get off.

I often wonder if some of the many activities our family is involved in aren't just keeping us going around in circles like Patrick on the carousel. Or are they truly helping us grow in holiness? I have to stop myself to ask if what I am doing is bringing my family closer to Christ. Sometimes I get so wrapped up in what I am doing that I fail to see it's time to stop and get off. Excuses like, "It's fun." "We enjoy it." or "It's what everyone else is doing." are not good enough reasons to keep doing the things that are taking us nowhere.

The Lord has taught me to look for signs that I need to decrease the amount of activities my family is involved in. One of the biggest signs is when our family evening prayer time gets pushed out of our schedule or shoved back so late that the kids can hardly stay awake, let alone focus on prayer. That is a sure sign to me that it is time to pull back a little and reprioritize. Another is when we can't seem to get everyone together for supper as a family. So many activities conflict with this time of day, and yet it is such a beautiful time to listen to my children as they share their simple joys and tearful trials. It is a time for Mark and me to help them see Christ in their day and to teach them their faith. Mark once asked one of his classes to write one thing they wished they could have. More than one student wrote that they would just once like to have their family together for dinner. I would imagine their parents would write the same.

Patrick loves being on a carousel, but eventually I have to pry him off the ride if he doesn't get off on his own. He isn't happy that I make him leave, but sometimes Mother knows best. Once at an amusement park, a worker told Patrick that he could stay on a spinning ride one more time. It's one of those rides that goes around while the seat simultaneously spins. Patrick was having a great time, but from the look on his face and the pale color of his skin, I knew it was time for him to get off. He had already gone around one too many times.

Like Patrick I am sometimes drawn to the fun and excitement of a ride that is taking me nowhere. It may even be making my family and me spiritually sick. In our crazy rush-around world it can be so hard to see what is really happening, and so I look to my heavenly Father for the grace I need. He is always there to help me recognize the carousels in my own life that I need to get off, and the many run-around activities I need to let go of. More than once, when I wouldn't budge, He has had to gently take me by the hand and lead me off the ride. He sets me down and points me in a different direction, one that leads only to Him.

"So, whether you eat or drink, or whatever you do, do all to the glory of God."
1 Corinthians 10:31

Chapter Sixteen

Let Go and Let God

August 29, 2002

Dear Patrick,

You've been back in school for a few weeks. I know how hard it is for you because I see the frustration on your face when I come to visit your classroom. Your art teacher, Mr. Willis, is a really special person. He has such patience, and I can tell you like him a lot. We have been so blessed to have caring, kind people to work with you ever since you started school. I can't believe this is your tenth school year, but it is. My thoughts go back to all the different schools and programs you've attended. You've had so many changes, Patrick, but you still keep trying.

It has been a good summer. I have missed being with you as much as I was last spring. I haven't been able to stay with you after my back surgery, and it doesn't look like I will be able to. I'll still see you at school every day, and we'll get to swim together at the YMCA a few times a week. Those are special times for me because I know how much you love the water, and the other kids love to go swimming with you too.

We continue to learn more and more about autism and ways to help you. There is so much to read and so much to learn. I pray that many breakthroughs in autism will come about through research and clinical studies. More and more children are being afflicted with this disorder, and no one seems to know why.

We have to start daily allergy shots for the next month with you now. I wish there were some other way, but the doctor thinks this is the best way to build you up to maintenance level. Then we can back off to one shot a week. We've also been meeting with your behavioral specialists to try to learn more effective ways to help you deal with your aggression. We're trying to do all we can to make you as healthy and happy as possible. We hope and pray that you get to the point where you can come back home to stay with us. That has always been our goal through all of this, and it is still our daily wish and prayer. I keep telling you that, and I hope you understand. God bless you, Buddy.

I love you,
Dad

"Therefore do not be anxious about tomorrow, for tomorrow will be anxious for itself. Let the day's own trouble be sufficient for the day."
Matthew 6:34

Always, one of the most difficult parts of being a father has been relinquishing control of our children to someone else's care. It's probably an extension of relinquishing my own will to the Will of the Father. I've never left any of the kids with a family member, friend, or babysitter when I didn't wonder how they were going to be while we were gone. Would they need me? Would something terrible happen? During those times when Patrick was young and could be left with a sitter for a few hours so that Beth and I could attend youth group or Basic Christian Community meetings, I was always happy to round the corner to see our house still standing with no signs of emergency vehicles in the driveway. Believe me, it was hard enough when those vehicles arrived when I was home with Patrick. Yes, we've had our share of visits from local law enforcement agencies.

As the children got old enough to go to school—first Sean, then Laura—my whole view of teaching changed. I realized that each of the 25 or 30 students in my classroom was loved deeply by someone at home. These parents (or in some cases grandparents) were entrusting their sons and daughters to my care for a part of every school day. More than ever I realized what an incredible responsibility I had to guide and direct my students. It wasn't easy for me to have Sean and Laura away, so I know it had to be even more difficult for Beth who was used to being with them all day. They would be fine, however, because they would make friends, could follow directions, and enjoyed being in school. I could reflect upon my own experiences and realize that everything would be o.k.

Such was not the case with Patrick. With Patrick I was reasonably sure that things were rarely o.k. As he started school in developmental programs, I had different expectations. As Beth has shared on several occasions, the love and concern shown by his special needs teachers encouraged me to believe that they had Patrick's best interests at heart. This was the beginning of the notion that I wasn't going to be able to do everything for my children.

Each step of Patrick's journey through school has been fraught with indecision. Is this the best place for him? Should we look into other programs? What about his medication? Is it helping or hurting? We've wondered about virtually every decision we've had to make. It's never been easy. For so long, I knew so little about what was best for him that I nearly blindly accepted whatever the educational professionals would offer. For sure, they had Patrick's best interests in mind, but they were often paralyzed by the reality of the scarcity of services and service providers. Plus they had many other students who needed similarly intensive care. I found myself more often praying that Patrick would be O.K., praying that he would receive what was best for him, and praying that I could trust the teachers, therapists, and doctors to know what was best for my son.

Patrick was nine when we moved to Loogootee, Indiana from Carmel, Indiana, and I really had no idea how the move would influence him. Neither did I know how it would change the rest of the family. I did have a very clear sense that God was calling my family to move back to my hometown though it made little sense to anyone who knew us. I loved my job. I had a great teaching position in what arguably may be the best school district in our state. With the help of friends and family, we had recently remodeled our home to better accommodate Patrick's needs. We had friends whom we could turn to for anything at any time. We attended Mass in a parish that had become an extended family and that I dearly loved. I served as president of the parish religious education council, and together Beth and I worked with the church's youth group. Conveniently, the parish had a 6:30 A.M. Mass that I was able to attend on my way to school. On the surface it made little sense especially when I considered that the position I had been offered paid much less than my previous position. Times like this are when it gets hard to be a husband and father.

Whatever I decided was going to determine the fate of my family and me. How woefully inadequate I am to make such decisions! The genesis of this move had been some six months before when I returned to my home parish of St. John to be a part of a "seed team" for Christ Renews His Parish, a weekend retreat program. I made my way from the parish center where the retreat was being held across Church Street to make a late night visit to the Blessed Sacrament on the second evening of the retreat. As I opened the glass doors separating the vestibule from the main church, I heard these words from within, "You are home. This is your home." I immediately sensed that God wanted me to return to my hometown though I can assure you I had never entertained the thought previously. Returning home from the retreat I had sat down at breakfast on Monday morning and simply called out to my wife, "Beth." Her response chilled me. "Where are we moving?" I hadn't told her about my visit in church or my feeling that God was calling me away from Carmel. I replied, "Who said we were moving anywhere?" As it happened I was looking at a newspaper article from my hometown paper, and a teaching position for which I qualified had opened.

Now that I had an offer for that position, one would think that I would be able to easily discern God's Will. I had heard God calling me home. I had interviewed for and been offered the position, but still I was looking for that silver platter with an absolutely clear answer. It didn't come. I had ten days to give the school district an answer, and I prayed like never before. A nearby church, St. Louis de Montfort, had a perpetual adoration chapel, and I visited it frequently. My fervent prayer was, "Lord, is this what you want of me? Is this your Will? Lord, I'm not sure I want to do this. Really, I don't want to do this. Will you send me a sign?" If I had put that much prayer into all the decisions I have made, I no doubt would be a much happier, much more fulfilled person. Two days before I had to let the Loogootee School Corporation know my answer, I received a phone call from my dad and another from my brother, Bob. Both said they had felt God was telling them to call and that I should take the offer. Finally, I had enough "data" and accepted the job. The Lord had to work overtime on me.

Now, more than four years later, I still wonder what it's all about. I suppose none of us ever know completely why God brings us to where we are. Maybe I have spent too much time trying to figure it all out. Maybe I haven't spent enough. I don't know. I suspect that Patrick would have never gone to Silvercrest Children's Development Center had we stayed in Carmel. The schools there were excellent, and the state likely would not have approved it, as his programming was first-rate. Certainly, I never would have met so many wonderful people in my new parish, school, and town.

It is this search for and surrender to God's will that is so important. More and more I have accepted my limited human understanding. More and more I have accepted that, as a father, I cannot do everything and be everywhere for my children. I am much more dependent upon others and God than my foolish pride will allow me to accept. As Patrick moved into his own little house in a neighboring town, I had to realize this all over again. Simply stated, I cannot do what, I believe, is most often in the best interest of my son. I cannot provide a home for him that is the best possible environment to meet his needs. For a father like me, that is hard to accept. I want to believe that I can give my children exactly what they need when they need it.

The saving aspect of his move to a new home was that I was going to be able to be part of his support staff. I was going to be able to work with him and to stay with him several hours each week. That helped so much when we realized that Patrick had to move away again. And, it was wonderful. For the first two and a half months Patrick was in his new home, I was able to be with him often. That eased his transition, and, I hope, allowed him to know that he wasn't being abandoned. Mommy and Daddy and his brothers and sisters would still be a part of his life. It was great to be with him during those weeks. Then God's plan intervened. I had to have back surgery.

The hardest part of the surgery was knowing that I couldn't work with Patrick for at least six weeks. My doctor had told me that I couldn't be in a car for two weeks after the operation and that I wasn't allowed to pick up anything over ten pounds for four weeks after that. I wondered if Patrick would understand, and I surmised that he wouldn't. When I explained it all to him, I didn't see any hint of recognition. Patrick so much needs consistency, and now I wasn't going to be there for him. When he was at Silvercrest, the time between weekends when I could visit was always too long for me. I don't know if he could appreciate the passage of time, but I could. I hated the idea of being separated from Patrick for so long and being unable to do much to help my family because of my back problems. As I reflected on that these words came into my mind. "I will not abandon you. I will not leave your orphaned. I am here for you. I will be with Patrick." Once again, through prayer, I had the assurance of our Heavenly Father. It will be all right. It will work out for the best. I just have to keep doing my part, and God will do the rest. That is if I continue to seek His will.

"Truly I say to you, unless you turn and become like children,
you will never enter the kingdom of heaven."
Matthew 18:3

Chapter Seventeen

Soft, Gentle Words

October 21, 2002

My Dear Patrick,

It was great to be with you today when Jenny and I took you to the doctor. Jenny has always enjoyed working with you. She cares a great deal about you, and I can't count the times she has told me how much you have helped her to be a better person. You sure seemed to enjoy the little stop we made to have your picture taken. The one with the American flag behind you was so cute. You did a great job.

When we got to the doctor I was relieved to hear that your ear infection had cleared up completely. Two weeks ago when the doctor looked into your ears and saw an infection, I was so surprised. I guess the fact that you are constantly covering your ears makes it hard for us to know when the pain is from noise, and when it is from infection. You should feel much better now. God has always given us good doctors to help you, especially our family doctor, Dr. Hoffman.

It has been hard to get over to your house and spend time with you over the past month. I don't know if you remember, but Grandpa had triple bypass surgery in September, and Daddy and I have tried to be around to help out where we can. As always, it is hard not to be with you. At least your daddy gets to see you at school every day.

Back in September, on the 23rd, we got a phone call from a man named Denny who builds houses to rent. We've told you about him before. He said he would build a special little house for you that would fit your needs perfectly. He is going to make the ceilings high so you can jump up without hitting your head, no matter how tall you get. If you are anything like some of your uncles, you could be 6 feet, 6 inches some day. It will be a new house, so you won't have all the trouble with the mold and mildew that you have in the house you are in now. This time when he called he said he was ready to start building. He hopes to have you in your new house by maybe as soon as Christmas.

Even though you are in the next town over from us, you still seem so far away. We pray that your moving into the new house will bring you one step closer to moving home. We had a case conference last week at school, and it seems that things there have gotten worse. I know your frustration with not being able to communicate has a lot to do with it. So many people are trying very hard to help you. Please don't give up on us.

When Daddy tells me you had a good day at school it always makes me so happy. I have a hard time thinking of you confused, frustrated, or hurting. I want to make everything better, but I know I can't. I can't bring you home either. Only God can do that. God reminds me over and over again, that He has a plan and a special place for you.

On Sunday afternoon Laura will be confirmed. I wish you could be with us, but I think it will be just too much for you, and, as usual, there will be food around that you cannot eat. I don't know if you understand Confirmation, but it is a very special Sacrament. It is a time when Laura will receive special grace from the Holy Spirit to help her live her Catholic faith, even to the point of death. Some of your classmates will soon begin preparing for their own Confirmation next year. I wish you could be with them, and yet I truly believe that God is giving you all the grace to do what He wants you to do. He is preparing you for something special. For now I thank Him for the beautiful afternoon we spent together. Your brothers and sisters, Daddy, and I will be with you in a few days. Maybe we will go swimming. God bless you, my little one.

I love you,
Mommy

"But the fruit of the Spirit is love, joy, peace, patience, kindness, goodness, faithfulness, gentleness, self-control; against such there is no law."

Galatians 5:22-23

It was a calm, peaceful afternoon. Mark was on spring break from school, and so I had put him to work painting the girls' room. It was one of those sudden thoughts I get like, "Let's paint the girls' room" which translates into "Let's go now. I'll pick out the paint, and you can paint the room today." Grandma and Grandpa stopped by to play with the kids and were sitting off the dining room talking with Mark while he painted. Believe it or not, from our dining room you can easily talk to someone in any other room of our house.

As I walked into the kitchen to start dinner, Megan let out a scream. It was not a scream of terror. It was more like an "I don't know what to do" type of scream. This was quickly followed by a low, quiet, slightly irritated moan from Mark. As I turned I could see blue paint all over the floor of the girls' room. Megan had stepped in the pan of blue paint and then knocked it over. Somehow I was able to say in a soft voice, " It's O.K. It will clean up; just don't move, Megan."

I had to move quickly and quietly to get things under control or there would be a greater price to pay. I knew there was only one way to do it, and that was with lots of prayer and reminding myself that it was only paint. If I could get past the fact that it was seeping into the cracks of the wood floor, and that Megan's new jeans, the ones that still had tags on them, were now covered with paint, I could remain calm. Miraculously, all but a few specks of the paint came off the floor, and all the paint came out of her jeans. Most importantly, however, there were no harsh words, and no one was hurt.

Yelling, screaming, and strong, corrective words are forbidden in our home. I've had this rule since the day I brought my firstborn Sean home from the hospital, but I've never found a good way to enforce it, or follow it very well for that matter. I truly believe that kind, gentle words, spoken out of love are much more effective. Patrick has a way of helping us control our tongues. It is not a good way; in fact, we are trying everything we can think of to stop it. However, his method is working.

When someone says the word "no" or yells or screams in an angry way, Patrick has it in his mind that he has to hit someone. It usually is not even the person who screams, unless they are correcting Patrick. It may be a brother or sister three rooms away, but someone somewhere has to be hit. It can be as small as a tap, or it can be as great as throwing a child against the wall with one swing of his arm.

This has been very painful to see. Patrick usually does one of two things: he becomes very upset and starts to cry, which is usually followed by more hitting, or he responds like someone swatting a fly. That is, he acts as if nothing ever happened. Either way the entire family has learned a great deal of self-control regarding the way we speak to each other. It is as if God has given us a tangible, physical way to see the harm that our mouths can do to others and sometimes to ourselves.

I have to catch myself when Michael walks across the carpet with muddy shoes, and change what I might have said to a gentle, cheerful, "Michael, it would be great if you would take those shoes off before you walk across the floor." At nine, Michael already knows not to walk on the carpet with muddy shoes. He just needs reminders. The great part about this is that I have found my children actually listen to me and obey me much better when I talk to them with a pleasant voice. It's not easy, and from time to time a firm yet gentle hand is needed to point one of my children in the right direction.

When my thirteen-year-old son Brendan was about three he gave me a glimpse into Patrick's world that has helped tremendously. I was at a wallpaper store that had a playroom for children to use while parents shop. I let Brendan and Megan play with some of the toys while I looked at wallpaper. When it was time to go, I told them to put the toys away. Two-year old Megan started to put toys away, but Brendan stood by the door with a toy nearly identical to one we had at home. Over and over I asked him to put the toy away. I explained to him that his toy was at home, my voice growing stronger and firmer. I had to put the toy back myself, and then we headed out to the car. As I buckled Brendan into his car seat, my firm lecture continued. After a few short moments he looked up at me with his angelic face and pale blue eyes, full of questions and said, "Mommy, your eyes are angry, and your nose is angry, and your mouth is angry, and your eyebrows are angry, and your hair is angry." Then he stopped and just looked at me. My voice had become too irritating for him to listen to, and, needless to say, he hadn't heard a word I had said. All he knew was that his mother looked angry, and he didn't know why.

Brendan, while not autistic, suffers from a few of the same sensory issues that Patrick does. In fact I have learned many people do. Noise causes Brendan pain. It actually hurts his ears. Brendan has told us how hard it is to pay attention to anything when his ears hurt, and how he fears being yelled at. Playing baseball was quite a challenge, and as much as he loved it he could not tolerate the yelling from coaches and fellow players.

Fortunately, Brendan has learned to cope well with loud noises and hardly mentions it any more.

Patrick, though, still struggles. He wears earplugs often and covers his ears when he needs to. Once while we were in a restaurant with a play area Patrick was having a hard time with the noise, so he covered his ears. When his food came, he used his left hand to cover his left ear, and his right shoulder to cover his right ear. That way he could eat with his right hand. We've tried many expensive therapies and treatments over the years to try to desensitize his hearing, but we have never seen any notable improvement.

At this point, it is not so much the loud voices that lead Patrick to hit, as much as the tone of voice or the words used. No one likes being corrected, especially not Patrick. Where another child might protest or complain, Patrick hits to let us know he is not happy about what is being said, even if it is not directed toward him.

This has been a great trial for our family. It has been very hard to see my little ones in pain, crying as they run for their room to seek shelter from their brother. Mark and I frequently have had to hold Patrick while he cries, tears streaming down his face as he hits, kicks and pinches us. One comment that has helped me is from St. John of Avila who said, "I pray God may open your eyes and let you see what hidden treasures He bestows on us in the trials from which the world thinks only to flee."

This is a trial that our family does not want to flee. In fact, Patrick's brothers and sisters, at the risk of being hurt, have a hard time being away from him. He is very precious to us and we know God is blessing each one of us in ways we cannot imagine. For now, while Patrick is learning to control his hands and be gentle, we are learning to control our mouths. We are learning to use the kind of words God wants us to use, kind words, spoken out of love, words that don't hurt.

"Whoever humbles himself like this child, he is the greatest in the kingdom of heaven." Matthew 18:4

CHAPTER EIGHTEEN

In the Silence

November 20, 2002

Dear Patrick,

I know I say this a lot, but it is another confusing time. I thought we finally had a handle on things. I was convinced that the place for you was the new little house in Washington that Denny is building. I couldn't imagine anything better, but now I don't know for sure. It seemed so perfect. You could have a nice place that is free from the environmental problems in a safer location a few minutes closer to home. I know our area doesn't offer a lot of services that you need, but I couldn't imagine anything better.

Then Mommy and I went to Little Star Academy in Indianapolis to speak to a group of parents, and one of them began talking to us afterward. She is the mother of one of the boys we met at Heartspring in Kansas. Her name is Sherry Quinn. Her little boy is home from Wichita now, and she has such hope for him. She has a wonderful agency that helps children like you. She offered to help you if we could move you to the Indianapolis area. She started talking about many of the services that her son was receiving, and unfortunately, most of those services are not available in our small, rural area.

So now Mommy and I are confused again. Do we go ahead with the building process, or do we start looking elsewhere? We really need to pray for guidance, Patrick, because we want what is best for you. You seem to be getting no better at home or in school. In fact, it seems like you have regressed in some ways. I wish I could understand what is upsetting you so.

Patrick, Mommy and I love you so much. It hurts us when you can't share in the simple pleasures of the other children. They all just had a big overnight slumber party at Sr. Maria's house in Ferdinand and had a great time. There is no way you could do something like that. We want only what is best for you, but that is so hard to figure out. When we come to visit you at your house, you always seem to enjoy it, and yet you are eager to see us leave too. Is the commotion just too much for you to handle with your little brothers and sisters around? Are you as confused as we are? How I wish you could talk to us and tell us what you feel and think! That would seem to make everything so much easier. Of course, you cannot. God has made you in incredible and amazing ways, and I don't want you to change unless God wills it. And yet I long for the day I can hear your voice, when we can talk about how you are doing and what is best for us to do. I would love to know your opinions on things that affect you. Until then, I will keep praying for you and believing that God has an awesome plan for your life and that I must participate in that plan. Please know that I love you. God bless you, Patrick.

Love,
Dad

"Humble yourselves before the Lord and He will exalt you."
James 4:10

The life of St. Joseph of Cupertino is one of my favorite saint stories. Joseph was born in Cupertino, Italy in 1603. He had a very difficult childhood as his father, a poor carpenter, died prior to his birth. Like Jesus, he was born in what amounted to little more than a stable. By the age of 8 he was receiving ecstatic visions that left him staring off into space very much removed from the world. He received very little formal education and was rejected by the Friars Minors Conventuals. The Capuchins accepted him as a lay brother, but his ecstasies made it difficult for him to work. Finally, he was allowed to become an oblate at a Franciscan convent at about the age of 17. Despite his difficulties with learning, he was eventually ordained a priest at age 25. This in itself was miraculous as Joseph could barely read or write. He was gifted, however, with spiritual insights that allowed him to explain complicated theological or scriptural questions with relative ease.

In spite of Joseph's insights, others still often rejected him. He continued to receive ecstasies and even began levitating during prayer or while offering Mass. Prior to these miraculous events, Joseph was thought to be ignorant and useless by human standards. He was secluded from the outside world, was moved from convent to convent so as not to cause trouble, and even was brought before the Inquisition. Despite all these difficulties, Joseph retained his joyful demeanor. He died in 1663, was beatified in 1753 and canonized in 1767. I often encourage our children to pray for the intercession of St. Joseph when it comes to their schoolwork. When they are having difficulty learning, I know he can empathize.

I certainly don't claim that Patrick has any supernatural gifts or intelligence, but there is so much behind his eyes, within his silence, that I am certain something special is happening inside. Most often when Patrick and I go for walks or go to the park to play, we are completely silent. Patrick, of course, cannot speak, and while I generally talk to him when we are driving in the car or sitting at home, I usually don't say much on our walks. No doubt some of that is selfishness on my part. I crave quiet. Anytime I take Laura, Megan, Kate, Bridget, or Emily with me I can count on near constant chatter. My girls love to talk. And I love talking to my daughters, but I often long for silence. There is little solitude in the midst of my days with dozens of students at school and a waiting brood at home. It is different with Patrick.

I remember a day last summer when Patrick and I were going for a long walk through town. Patrick kept stopping to look at little things along the way: leaves, flowers, and bits of broken glass. He was going through a stage when he would genuflect every several steps. I have no idea why, but it was a perfect imitation of what one does when entering a pew at church. Several times on the walk after his genuflection or inspection of a leaf, he would turn around and grab my hands to squeeze and then look directly into my eyes. It was as if he were trying to communicate something through his actions. I was having difficulty keeping up with him that day because of a ruptured disk in my back that was shooting pain down my right leg, so these stops were welcome relief. My doctor had scheduled surgery for a few days later, and it couldn't come soon enough.

Each time he looked at me though I had a curious feeling. Somehow I could see beyond his eyes and could almost read his thoughts. I had been telling Patrick about my back condition for several days, but I had no reason to believe he understood me. Something, however, was different on this walk. As I looked into his eyes, I felt as if he knew I was hurting. I had the distinct feeling that everything was going to be all right after my upcoming surgery. Beth's aunt, Sister Maria Tasto, had a similar feeling with Patrick a few years ago while undergoing treatment for cancer. I can't explain it, but sometimes it's as if he understands another's pain. Perhaps it is because he has suffered so much himself.

Patrick's gazes into our eyes are brief. He rarely maintains eye contact for more than a few seconds. These glances, however, have become some of the most intimate communication that Beth and I have with Patrick. To me the spoken and written word is priceless. I spend a good portion of each day reading, studying, and teaching. To Patrick, words are often useless. He cannot use them, and he frequently doesn't seem to be able to comprehend them. True, he has gotten better about following verbal prompts over the years, but we still see a lot of confusion. He may pick up his coat when someone tells him to get his shoes, for example, or he may simply ignore the speaker altogether.

Like St. Joseph of Cupertino, Patrick's gifts are hidden. He will not likely add to our gross national product or become a productive member of our society's workforce. He may never play an instrument or score a winning goal. He may never have a girlfriend or marry. In fact, to the world, Patrick may seem as if he is nothing but a burden, but our family has been given so much through him. Our children are more sensitive to the needs of others because they have a brother with such severe needs. Through Patrick, they have been exposed to other children with disabilities, and it has allowed them to understand more clearly the many blessings God has given them. They have learned unconditional love for Patrick because, from a child's perspective, he usually does nothing to help them. More often, Patrick has broken their toys, torn up one of their keepsakes, or even hurt them physically. Yet, the children are drawn to him. They love him and know there is something special about him.

What Patrick possesses that eludes the rest of us is his holiness. Thank God he has the inability to sin. Our goal as parents is to provide for the emotional, social, physical, financial, and spiritual needs of our children. Chief among these needs is the spiritual. More than anything else, our desire is to lead our children to Heaven. Patrick is well on his way. He may never be canonized a saint like St. Joseph of Cupertino, but he will be among the saints in Heaven. That much I know. I pray that I may join him there, and that he helps lead many others into the Kingdom as well.

"Oh, Lord, our Lord, how majestic is Thy Name in all the earth! Thou Whose glory above the heavens is chanted by the mouth of babes and infants...."

Psalm 8:1-2

Chapter Nineteen

The Mirror

December 1, 2002

My Dear Patrick,

We missed not seeing you last weekend. We had to be out of town for a few events where Daddy and I were speaking. Many people are being touched by your story. It has been beautiful to hear their different reactions. I think the reason it helps them so much is because when they see how God has an awesome plan for your life, they also see He has one for theirs. As I often say, He is not a part-time God. As they see how precious you are to God through the many stories, they realize that they too are precious to Him. Patrick, He made each one of us to be perfect with him in Heaven, no matter how broken or hurting our bodies are here on earth. For now you are exactly the way God wants you, and you are beautiful. He also loves you so much that He won't leave you as you are. Each day He will help you to become more and more like Christ. Someday you will see.

While we were gone many beautiful things happened, but something very difficult also happened. Yesterday morning, Bridget woke up struggling to breathe. We were staying with Caeser and Jane. Since Jane and I are both nurses, we could tell she was having an asthma attack. We quickly got her to the hospital for help, but it was scary. Your cousin Eric struggled with asthma for many years. When he was 21, he died from an asthma attack. I'm sure you remember Eric. He was such a good person, and we have all missed him very much. That is why it scared me. Do you remember having an asthma attack when you were small? It was only one time, but it was very hard for you to breathe.

Bridget seems to be fine now. The doctor treated her with medication for a week, and she got well quickly. Only time will tell if she will suffer from asthma again. It has a lot to do with allergies, and we know, like you, she is allergic to dogs. What we don't know are all the other things she might be allergic to as well.

Daddy and I will be meeting with the team of people who help us take care of you this week. We have much to talk about, including getting you to the dentist and helping you with your allergies. We are trying to find ways to decrease the things around you that may irritate you. Maybe this way you will be able to tolerate situations better without becoming so upset. We are going ahead with the building of a new house for you in Washington. We do not know how long you will live there, but it seems for now that God wants you in your own little house in the woods. There have been some delays, and now it is scheduled to be ready by March. I pray this will help you. We are very excited. It is greater than we had ever dreamed possible.

We look forward to seeing you soon. Maybe some day we can take you with us when we travel. So many people would like to see you. You are an amazing and beautiful young man and I miss you so much. God bless you, my little one.

I love you.
Mommy

"For everything created by God is good, and nothing is to be rejected if it is received with thanksgiving; for then it is consecrated by the word of God and prayer."

1 Timothy 4: 4-5

For the first two years of Patrick's life, someone else had cut Patrick's hair. Now it was my turn. I was sure I could do it. I even had the style planned out in my head. First, I made sure he was happily eating crackers in his high chair. Then, with scissors in one hand and a comb in the other I made my attempt. For the first few seconds, Patrick sat very still, but then he decided he wanted to see what it was I was doing back there and what those snipping sounds were all about. This made for a very difficult situation. It wasn't long before I gave up all ideas about style and started cutting anything that stuck out and looked even remotely like hair. In the end I was on the floor holding Patrick with one hand and a clippers in the other. His new style was a very short buzz, not at all my intention.

When I finished, I took Patrick to the mirror to see for himself what I had done to him. I was irritated and covered in hair, and after the entire struggle his hair looked nothing like I had planned. My attitude changed, however, when I saw Patrick's reaction. He giggled and danced around as he ran his hands over his fuzzy head. He seemed to like what he saw. He actually liked the haircut I had given him. As he danced in front of the mirror making faces, my attitude changed. His joy became my joy, and I couldn't help but smile.

Patrick has always liked mirrors. Over the years we've seen Patrick's many faces dance before the mirror. When Patrick was in preschool the class dressed up like bunny rabbits, and the teacher used a washable black marker to make their noses black like little bunnies. After that educational experience, Patrick decided that black mascara works just as well. I can't count the times I have found him in my bathroom with a black nose jumping in front of the mirror. Also, Patrick loves to try on hats in front of the mirror too. Just about any hat will do. His favorite used to be Grandpa Gibbons' fishing hat, but that has fallen apart. Now he loves wearing Mark's brown cap. He will even turn things that aren't hats, like an Easter basket or a pair of shorts, into hats to see how they look. It doesn't seem to matter what it is, as long as he can get it on his head, he runs for the mirror to see how it looks.

When Patrick is unhappy, he also goes to the mirror. When he was little, the mirror was always a place for joy and fun. He always liked what he saw and laughed or giggled at his image as he made goofy faces. As he has gotten older though the mirror has occasionally become a place for frustration and pain. We have gone through many mirrors in the past few years because he has broken them in frustration. We're never quite sure why. The hard part is not replacing the broken ones; it is seeing him in front of the mirror, his eyes full of pain and tears. We don't know what causes him to be upset and hit the mirrors. I've wondered sometimes if, maybe for a brief moment, he wants to be different. As happy as Patrick usually is when he looks at himself, perhaps there are those times when he doesn't like what he sees. Maybe it is because he doesn't think we can see who he really is.

As I think about Patrick looking at himself, I wonder about what I see when I look at myself, when I look at what God has given me. Do I act like Patrick when he was little, happy with what I see? My usual reaction is not one of gratitude to God for the eyes that can see, the mouth that can talk, the nose that can smell, and the ears that can hear. What I see is how imperfect I look in comparison to the flawless faces I see on the cover of magazines. I find myself wishing I looked different than I do instead of thanking God for what He has given me.

When Mark and I were engaged, I decided to knit him a scarf. First, however, I had to learn how to knit. Once I did I chose the perfect black yarn and began to make this very special gift. When I gave it to him, he was delighted. I can't imagine how I would have felt if he would have said, "I like it, but it would be better if the yarn were blue and if it wasn't so big. You know I really like scarves that are made by machine. They probably cost less at stores than what it cost you to make this." I would have been crushed, and yet a scarf is small compared to the gift of life God has given to me.

Watching Patrick in front of the mirror has helped me to be grateful for who I am, for the body God has carefully chosen to give me out of love. I've tried to extend this gratitude to include all the gifts God has given me including my worn down house with crayon on the walls, molding falling off, and clutter in the closets. Mother Teresa once told my uncle, Father John, "If God puts you in a palace, live there and be happy, and if the next day he puts you in the street in a cardboard box, live there and be happy. When you live in the palace, don't want for the streets, and when in the streets, don't want for the palace."

When I find myself irritated over the condition of our house, I try to turn that irritation into praise that I have a house, and not only that, but thank God that my house is in poor condition because it is full of beautiful children on their way to heaven. One child, in particular, makes us all smile when he laughs and dances in front of the mirror.

"Because you are precious in my eyes, and honored, and I love you, I give men in return for you, people in exchange for your life."

Isaiah 43:4

Chapter Twenty

Running the Race

December 25, 2002

Dear Patrick,

Another year has almost passed. It's Christmas night, and you weren't home with us today. In the middle of the afternoon, I came over to your house with Megan, Brendan, and Michael while Mommy and the rest of the kids stayed at home. We had six inches of snow last night, and I just can't drive the old van in the snow. It slips and slides all over the place, and I didn't want to risk getting stuck in the snow with all the kids. Mommy wanted to come over so badly, but she had to stay at home with the little ones.

It was wonderful to have you with us at Christmas Eve Mass. I was really happy that Jenny could bring you. You looked really sharp in your new brown pants and sweater. You seemed really interested in all the lights on the Christmas trees and were well behaved. What a blessing that was for all of us! We even had a couple people tell us after Mass that it was really special to see you there with the rest of us.

It has been hard the last week and a half. Grandpa Matthews died on December 15th, and you didn't seem to understand when I told you about it. He has been sick for a while and just couldn't hold on any longer. Mommy and I were out of town at a book signing in Carmel. I was talking to some old friends from Our Lady of Mt. Carmel when Mommy walked into the room with Caeser and told me that Grandpa had died. Patrick, he died on the third Sunday of Advent, Gaudete Sunday. It's a day that we are reminded of a reason to rejoice for the coming of Jesus into the world. If it weren't for Jesus' coming, Grandpa wouldn't be able to go to heaven. Neither would you or I.

Patrick, Grandpa Matthews loved you so much. He was always willing to help out with you in whatever way he could. Grandpa used to love to watch you run, jump, and swing. Do you remember sitting on that big tree stump by the garden and watching Daddy and Grandpa? That's one of my favorite memories of you two together. He asked me how you were doing just about every time I talked to him, and he was interested in whatever we were trying to accomplish with your latest therapy or treatment. He was really excited about the possibility of you getting a new house to live in, one that fit your needs so much better. We talked about that possibility a lot. I got a little scared in the last couple of years as Grandpa was getting older and more frail because you would still try to jump on him and get him to play with you. I know you didn't realize that it was hard for Grandpa to try to hold you or play with you.

What would I like you to remember about your grandpa? First of all, he was a man of deep faith. He prayed for you and all of his family every day. Grandpa loved going to Mass and praying the rosary. His Catholic faith was very important to him, and that faith motivated him to serve others. Grandpa was a founding member of the St. Vincent De Paul Society in our parish and was a member for fifty years. Through that organization he was able to help the poor and visit the sick and lonely. He taught me and my brothers and sister through his actions. We learned that God comes first in our lives, and that we need to serve others to be happy. We learned about the importance of family and the virtues of hard work, honesty, and integrity. Patrick, all the things that my dad taught me are things that I want to pass on to you and your brothers and sisters. I just wish you could understand all this.

Patrick, Mommy and I didn't know whether or not you should go to the funeral home to see Grandpa's body. We thought you probably should be there with the rest of the kids. I hoped it would help you to realize that Grandpa won't be around anymore. When we did bring you in to see Grandpa's body, it was so hard. I don't know if it was all the people or the smell of the flowers, or if it was just not your normal after-school routine, but you got so upset. I hope it was the right thing to do. I just didn't want to leave you out. As much as Grandpa helped you while he was with us, we have the hope that Grandpa will be able to help you more from heaven. Now, he can intercede for us as a member of the Church Triumphant and can look over us in a whole new way.

We are coming near the end of another year, Patrick, and we still don't know what the future holds. Next year you may be able to get into a new house that better meets your needs, or we may find that we have to move you someplace farther away from us, so that you can get the therapy that is best for you. It's so hard to know what to do. We keep praying and hoping that we make the right decisions. I guess the important thing is that we don't give up. We have to keep trying to decide what God wants for you, Patrick. I know he has an awesome plan for you and for us.

I love you, Patrick.
Daddy

"In this you rejoice, though now for a little while you may have to suffer various trials, so that the genuineness of your faith, more precious than gold which though perishable is tested by fire, may redound to praise and glory and honor at the revelation of Jesus Christ."

1 Peter 1:6-7

I'm not the best childcare provider. In fact, I'm still somewhat impaired in child rearing. As the youngest of seven children, I didn't have very many opportunities to take care of small children. Beth probably changed more diapers by the age of eight than I have in my whole life. Still, I was at the point where I thought I had it all together. Through the years I think I had learned to be a pretty good dad. It was one of those perfect warm summer evenings. Beth had gone to a hair appointment to get a hair cut, and I had complete charge of the gang. No problem, right?

Early in our marriage, this would have been a time for a lot of stress. I learned how to take care of Sean, Laura, and Patrick "on the job." We were living in California, and Beth had a job working twelve-hour weekend shifts at a hospital in Hemet. Sean was three, Laura was two, and Patrick was about four months old. I was apprehensive those first few Saturday mornings, but Beth seemed to have confidence in me, and her sister Mary was close by to help out. I kept telling her that I didn't know what I was doing. Sean was just getting to the point where I could relate to him. He would respond to questions, would throw a ball back and forth, and shared my love for Saturday morning cartoons. Laura was developing quickly and could do many of the same things as Sean. Plus, she was just darn cute.

Then there was Patrick. I don't know if I am like most men or not, but I just don't have a yearning or desire to hold small babies. It's not my natural instinct to walk up to a baby with arms out. I'll hold one of our little ones for a few minutes, but then I'm ready to pass him or her off to a willing set of arms. Fortunately, these days there are many willing recipients.

By the time Patrick was ten, though, it was all old hat. I had "been there and done that" and was feeling pretty confident. The kids had gathered around me in my favorite recliner to hear a chapter of C.S. Lewis's *The Chronicles of Narnia.* With three or four on my lap and the bigger ones clinging close by, I read to them with my best Aslan voice. We were just getting to an exciting part when I did a quick head count. Patrick wasn't listening to the story, but he had been close by. He was running around the living room and jumping on the couch. We must have gotten particularly engrossed in the story because none of us realized that Patrick had slipped off.

"Sean, Laura, where's Patrick?" I don't know how many times I've asked that or a similar question. "I don't know, Dad. I didn't notice he was gone." I wish I could say that he had never disappeared before, but that is just not true. We quickly fanned out for a search of the house. He wasn't in either bathroom; we didn't find him in bed; he wasn't in the basement. I began frantically combing the backyard looking down toward the creek. Quite frequently Patrick would be walking across a big tree that had fallen across the creek, but I didn't see him there. Sean, Laura, and Brendan began searching the field and creek in front of the house. About ten minutes into my hectic search, Beth drove up the driveway.

"What's going on?" she asked. "Patrick is missing again. We've been checking everywhere, and I have no idea where he is. I think he's been gone about fifteen or twenty minutes." With Beth home, I was able to leave her with the rest of the kids as I did a quick search of the neighborhood pools. Patrick was still drawn to the water, but the creek usually was where he found relief. Not so tonight. I quickly determined that he wasn't in any of the neighbors' pools, so I climbed into our car and began combing our subdivision.

It was getting dark, and I was worried. I slowly drove up and down the streets hoping someone was taking a walk or finishing up yard work, but no one was out. Our subdivision is rather large, and it's nearly a half mile to Bloomfield Road, the main thoroughfare. It seemed like a long time, but I'm sure it was a mere few minutes until I found Patrick. There he was: barefoot, in his underwear, running, head down, toward the main road. I have no clue where he thought he was going, but he was determined to get there. I stopped the car, jumped out, and yelled, "Patrick! Stop!" I could have been just as easily yelling at the trees because he didn't even pause. I began running after him and stopped him just before he made his way out onto the main road, not even bothering to look for oncoming traffic.

Exhausted and relieved, I paused just long enough to whisper a quick prayer. "Thank you, Lord," I huffed. I looked into Patrick's deep brown eyes and saw not a hint of recognition or relief. As usual, he acted as if he had no idea what all the fuss was about.

I wish I had his determination. Patrick was intent upon getting somewhere. I was reminded of St. Paul's admonition to the Hebrews, " Therefore, since we are surrounded by so great a cloud of witnesses, let us lay aside every weight, and sin which clings so closely, and let us run with perseverance the race that is set before us, looking to Jesus the pioneer and perfecter of our faith" (Hebrews 12:1-2). St. Paul was speaking about the Communion of Saints. I recalled how often I had called upon the saints to help me with Patrick, my special little runner. St. Therese of Lisieux, the Little Flower, is someone to whom I've had a special devotion. She often spoke of spending her time in eternity doing good on earth, and I've asked her to protect Patrick many times. After Beth's dad, Don, died I began asking him to help look after Patrick too. He loved to push him on the swings and follow him around the yard when Patrick was a toddler, and I was sure he would be of even greater help now. I don't know if it was St. Therese, Don, or some others, but Patrick had once again been preserved to run another day.

As a father, it is very hard to accept that I cannot do everything for my children. I want to protect them, provide for them, and teach them. But I can't do it alone. It's been a difficult lesson to learn. I've been far too proud of doing everything on my own. Patrick has taught me—very slowly—to seek the help of others. So many people have showered my family with gifts of food, time, money, and a watchful eye. It's humbling for me, but I need whatever takes a whack at my pride. It is part of what, I hope and pray, will prepare me for my heavenly home.

God has a special place for Patrick and for each of us. That special place is where He has put us right now with all of its difficulties and struggles, with all of its joys and triumphs. God has placed people in our lives to challenge us, to strengthen us, and to be Christ to us. He has given us intellect, talents, and treasure to serve Him right where we are. Tomorrow it may change, but we don't have to concern ourselves with that. Today has enough concerns of its own.

Ever since Patrick went away to the residential school our one desire has been to bring him back home. It is the desire of each of our hearts to seek home. God allowed Patrick to return home for a while, but he had to leave again all too soon. He still has so much to learn, so much to overcome, so much to teach us. Maybe some day our desires will be fulfilled. Maybe someday he will be back home with us, but there is something of much greater importance. What is more important for Patrick and for all of us is that we make our way to our heavenly home. That alone is our ultimate desire. That is the place for you and the place for me.

"And when I go and prepare a place for you, I will come again and will take you to myself, that where I am you may be also."
John 14:3